WINTER

{effulgences, devotions}

Sarah Vap

Book Cover Design: Alban Fischer
Book Interior Design: Sarah Gzemski

Published by Noemi Press, Inc. A Nonprofit Literary Organization.
www.noemipress.org.

WINTER

{effulgences, devotions}

Sarah Vap

Death takes place in my very being—how can I explain to you?

Clarice Lispector

Winter

Snow is falling, a fire is burning in the fireplace, something is baking, the family-animal is cozy inside—

I am unable to sufficiently imagine the.

Winter

Glut, I.

The noise in this cabin—my brains exploding from noise—the slams.

Screeching, laughing, crying. Rain on the roof. Sonar pinging at each moment into our brains—

into the brains of whales—and all the other sea creatures—this animal asleep in my arms—

love made a body—for a complete mind. I

Winter, a possible beginning

It is 3 o'clock in the morning. It is raining hard. I am nursing Oskar in front of the fire. His eyes are closed and he's reflexively nursing as he falls asleep—one-two-three, pause, one-two-three, pause.

There are boxes all around us. We're moving into our new home—a little cabin with a creek behind it on the Olympic Peninsula of Washington. We're six miles away from the narrow fjord of the Salish Sea called Hood Canal. I have never, in all my life, heard rain falling as hard as it is falling right now.

The fire in front of us periodically shifts or flares when wind blows down the chimney. There is a blanket wrapped around us. The sound of rain is filling the cabin, and a gust of wind blowing rain at the window just woke Oskar. He is completely peaceful, and now also completely awake, in the middle of the night.

He is staring unblinkingly—right now—into my soulface while he nurses again. Now he is drinking deep—the milk has just come in again, and milk is running down his chin as he gulps and stares, stares, stares into my eyes and right now we are the same thing as each other.

Firelight flickers on the ceiling, on the walls, on his face—he looks exactly how he feels to me—full of light.

I don't know how much time has passed in front of this fire—he is asleep again in my arms. What does Oskar believe was the beginning of his time.

What does Oskar believe that I.

Winter, several years later

Oskar and Mateo are asleep upstairs with their father. The rain stopped, but the wind is blowing.

The longevity of this profoundest interruption, I.

I am now several years into this practice of trying to write a poem about winter during the pieces of time I find to be alone. Usually very early in the morning. Almost always at this desk. Sometimes I have just a few seconds before they wake. Sometimes I get an hour, but during that hour I am usually so dispersed that all I can do is find a phrase or two, the beginning of a path back to my mind.

Since the first baby was born, my torso—from the base of my throat to the tip of my vulva, from my shoulder points to my hip points, down my sternum and out through all the ribs attached to it, each of the ligaments connected to each vertebrae down my spine, and all of my organs—has the feeling of having been turned inside-out, and then everything pulled or dropped or ripped or spilling out of me.

And then my whole torso was pushed right-side in again, and all the pieces pushed or shoved back inside, to resemble something of what the torso was before the children.

I've been drained of. Then re-filled with too much, I.

And my mind has the feeling of having just been exploded.

Or this is another way of thinking about it—since the babies were born, my brains have the feeling of having been shot-through several times—and the bullets have opened tunnels through my brains.

And the tunnels—they have bored through my coherence, I.

Winter

This morning, snow.

Imagine: everything that was once inside of my brains is—right now—pouring out of my brains.

Imagine: everything pouring out. The bullets have just tunneled through my brains, so

memories are pouring out of my brains, longing is pouring out of my brains, what I've previously thought of as my self is pouring out of my brains, what I've learned across the years is pouring out of my brains, all the things I've done right and wrong are pouring out of my brains.

Then, imagine that into those emptied-out brain-tunnels, other things immediately flow back in—and too many.

Love for the babies flows back into the holes in my brains, but the love is actually: awe.

The love is praise, wonder, overwhelm, glut, joy, fabulousness, sensation, fragility.

The love for the babies is a tenderness so extreme that its tentacles—it's a tenderness to insanity, I.

The love for the babies is actually a deep anxiety, and a hyper-vigilance.

Love for the babies is actually a cellular-level internalizing of the world's dangers. Dangers that are emanating from everywhere, dangers that are surrounding us—right now—

clouds of invisible danger, like wifi. Like viruses. Like snowfall.

Like naval and industrial sonar that pings into the brains of whales. Whales that are swimming in the waters around the peninsula that we are living on, right now.

Sonar that pings also into my brains. Sonar that pings into the brains of the babies.

Pings also into the brains of the head that is floating inside me, right now.

Winter

I woke early. So that I could be alone. So that I could write the crucial thing.

I moved the new baby's arm from off my throat. I moved the bigger baby's head off my leg.

They both wake up as I am doing this so I lie back down until they fall asleep again.

I try to get out of bed again, so that I can be alone—in order to write the crucial thing.

Their father comes into the kitchen to say why am I clanking the cup! he's so tired.

I turn on the computer. I sit down with my small cup of coffee, very strong with a little cream, when my oldest son wakes up and comes into the room to talk to me about the American Revolutionary War for a while, he is so interesting! Go back to bed love it's 5 a.m. okay mama.

Then the baby wakes up, and he is sitting on my lap right now. And right now he hits the cup of coffee out of my hand and onto the notebook I.

Then their father comes back into the room to point out that I didn't wake up again last night after I nursed the baby to sleep so he had to watch the movie *by himself*.

Now the baby sitting on my lap is punching my boob because he's so pissed at me for getting out of bed before he got out of bed.

Now their father tries to put pants on him because he won't get off my lap until he has pants on, but actually he doesn't want pants on, so now I'm a little mad at their father for trying to put pants on a kid who doesn't want to wear pants at this particular time—but I also want this kid off my lap.

Now the middle kid is on my lap, too. He is laughing about the pants that the baby doesn't want on.

Now the baby is hitting the middle kid in the face because Don't laugh at me! and the baby just really hurt him.

Their father sits down at his computer to write his crucial thing. There are two kids on my lap, both of them are crying.

There are no kids on his lap, and now one of them is yelling pancakes in my face. Is the crucial thing I.

Winter

This one was taken from one of several notebooks that I kept during these years. Written sometime during our first year on the peninsula. In it, only Oskar's been born. It would be a more peaceable beginning for this book: infant, music, sparseness:

This morning it's so cold that I've turned on the space heater as well as stoked the fire. Oskar and his father are both asleep upstairs. I can't tell if it's raining or snowing. I haven't looked yet.

Yesterday I thought I heard Oskar say "a tumor of snow." When I asked him to repeat what he'd said, he said to me, quoting Song of Songs, what I often say to him: "I love to look at you."

Breakfasts, tidying, exhaustion—all the regular things have come into my life since Oskar's come into my life—I think I hear him moving or speaking upstairs but I have a cold, so my hearing is worse than usual.

My mishears when my hearing aids aren't in are something that I've always believed in, but my mishears combined with his baby neologisms and phrasings are divinatory messages that I—yes, he's already awake.

Let me hear his delicious voice—I am a wall and my breasts are towers. But for my child, I am a city of peace.

Winter, my mind.

Oskar is now toddling. Oskar is now talking. Oskar now holds
my hand and walks in the rain and the snow. Oskar is tenderness
incarnate—his sense of humor, his love of animals.

Mateo is still an animal curled up inside of my chest—a snail attached
to the bottom of my lung.

At each of its points, the baby is a new dimension—or: now I perceive
symbiosis.

My children will be born into *this* world. I have never been in so much
danger.

I have never been so. I have never been so.

I have never been more.

I have never been as.

I'm still trying to discern the.

Transcription of a few minutes in our apartment in Abidjan, Ivory Coast, a few years later

Stop kicking him in the face. Stop it now. Ow. Do you hear me? No, it's not a game. He doesn't think it's a game. Don't bite me! I am sorry you are mad, but you can't have a pen if you write on the wall. Look at me: can you hear my words? You: sit here. You: over there. Get off of him, he doesn't like it. Look at his face: he doesn't like it. Get off me. You're choking me. I don't like it. Let go of his hair. If you flip him over like that he could bash his head into the side of that couch—we have told you many times not to do that. You can't forget not to hit—you have to remember. You: into your room to calm down. Are you ready for bed? Don't throw those. Don't throw anything in here. Of course it hurts, but you started the game. Ow. Ow. Why am I not listening to you? Because you started the game and you knew someone would get hurt. Are you ok? Hey: pen on paper only. Don't write on anything but paper. Will you get that from him? Quick, it's in his mouth. Don't touch me. No more touching me today. Go. GO. Let go of him. No one touch anyone else. Did you just do that? Don't climb on that. You have never been allowed to climb on that. That can fall over. You're not his parent, only a parent should move him off that. I can't hold you right now. I can't hold all of you at the same time. I'll hold him, then him, then you. You are after him. After. Wait ten minutes, I will hold him for ten minutes, then I will hold you for ten minutes. Will you brush his teeth, or do you want to floss the other one? Get the pen. No writing on the couch. Only write on paper. Stop grabbing him. Stop grabbing me. Don't hit! If you run past him and push him he will fall over. Remember how little he is. Falling hurts him. Hug him more gently. He's saying stop, so stop it. You can't squeeze him that hard. Don't hit. Not even with something soft. Watch out for the corner, if he steps back he will trip. How can we help you remember not to hit? I can't hear over the screaming. Please stop screaming in my ear. Don't scream in his ear either. Don't stand on my stomach. Your knee is on my neck. Now it's on my throat. Change the game. Change the game now. Can you get this one? Get him off me, please. Grab him before he falls off that. Yes, I see. Yes: I see you. Yes: I see it. Not right now. No. Not right now because I'm doing the last thing you asked me to do. How many arms do you see on my body? Two, that's right! And do you see that they are full? Not in here, you can do that outside, but you can't do that in here.

Winter, the beginning

Snow is falling right now. A fire is crackling in the fireplace. I am in our cabin on the Olympic Peninsula in the north-west corner of the United States while somewhere—far away from where I am—drones are probably killing someone right now.

There is a pretty rug in front of the fire, and there are two bookshelves behind me. The bookshelves are mounted on the wall over two low built-in cabinets. They're made of a dark-stained wood—I don't know enough about wood to say what kind of wood they have been constructed from, but the family that lived here before us built everything that I can see from where I sit, including the cabin itself. The cabin and everything in it are made from wood, and the cabin is in the middle of the woods.

My desk is small, also made of wood. It faces a little window, and when the leaves have fallen from the trees, I can see the bend of the creek. If the window is open in autumn, I can hear the thrashing of the spawning salmon, and I can smell their decaying bodies from my desk.

The forested mountains around this cabin are filled with logging roads, and every day logging trucks filled with the bodies of trees leave this valley. The trees will be turned into lumber—all these different forms of wood around me, right now.

We moved from Phoenix to this cabin on the Olympic Peninsula just a few days after Oskar turned one. We'd finished our MFA degrees at Arizona State University. My first two books had just been published simultaneously by different presses, weeks before. I hadn't given any readings from them. I hadn't promoted them. And I hadn't applied for any university teaching jobs that I was now technically qualified for. I defended my thesis, Todd defended his thesis, we threw a first birthday party for Oskar, then packed the car and left.

I was new to the peninsula, but I'd grown up in Missoula, Montana, an eight-hour drive to the east. Todd, though, was very deliberately returning home—to what those who are from here refer to not as the Olympic Peninsula, but as *Mason County*. His family, as he often says, is "Mason County, six generations, both sides." He is ingrained in this community, in this landscape. He shares in a collective family memory that includes each turn of every road we drive. Every body of water here—the estuaries, the bays, the coves, the lakes, the rivers, the creeks, the rocky beaches, the waterfalls, the bridges, the reservoirs— contain his specific memories, and his family's memories. I knew a few minutes into meeting him that if we were going to be together, I would be living in Mason County.

When we arrived we'd intended to get jobs teaching at a community college, and we'd intended to stay forever. We felt like it was meant to be and that the invisible world was looking out for us when we found this cabin that I am sitting in right now—

Todd, Oskar and I stayed in Todd's parents' basement while we looked for our own place. One afternoon we attended a Mason County Historical Society Meeting with Todd's grandma and aunt, and the "meeting" was a group of people gathering mushrooms in the mountains above the Skokomish Valley while Todd's dad, Mike, the local historian, in his camouflage pants, baseball cap and torn t-shirt, talked about the history of logging in the valley. After the meeting, returning to Mike and Lindy's house, we took a spontaneous right turn after descending the mountain's logging roads. Oskar slept in his car seat behind us. It was a sunny day in August. We drove a few minutes until we arrived at the last house at the end of the valley road. There was a For Sale sign on the closed front gate.

From the gate we could see that the cabin had a little red barn behind it, a greenhouse just large enough for seedlings, two enormous garden plots, six rows of raspberry canes to the side of one garden, an open shed, one horse in the field, a children's playhouse under a giant red cedar, and a small creek bending in a half-circle around the back of the cabin. Mountains within the adjacent Olympic National Forest curled around the property, and the front of the cabin faced down the length of the valley— a narrow farming valley divided in two by the Skokomish River—a river locally-famous for flooding so regularly that salmon swim across the road as part of their ancestral routes to spawning grounds farther up the valley.

We timed our drive from the cabin back to the mouth of the valley, where the river emptied into the backward J-shaped body of water called Hood Canal, a fjord of the Salish Sea—twelve minutes.

And then just a few more minutes along Hood Canal to arrive again at Mike and Lindy's house. We called the phone number on the For Sale sign, we heard the price, which seemed surprisingly affordable compared to what we were paying for our bug-filled apartment in Phoenix. We learned there were ten acres and that a second, much larger river-sized creek ran through the property beyond the field with the horse in it.

Todd's grandma, my parents, and Todd's parents all contributed toward the minimum down payment. We signed the papers around the time that the crisis in subprime mortgages began to affect the credit markets. Then the stock markets sank. Then adjunct teaching jobs in western Washington, and all over the country, began to disappear, and to rescind benefits like health care insurance. We moved into the house, now worth much less than we'd just paid for it, in October—as the rains were gaining momentum. We were so happy.

It is difficult to know where or how to begin arranging these pieces when one is trying to make a book with multiple threads of contemplation that have run from one's childhood to one's present. It is difficult to find a form within this book to accommodate the thousand scraps of paper, the fragments in journals, and the scattered files across three computers.

It is difficult when one wants, in this day and age, to contemplate innocence, the soul, happiness, babies, human love, paradox, a maternal body, and the scales of violence and intimacy.

And to attempt to remember, across this book, that the wars that have occurred during my lifetime have always been invisible to me.

A book about how to remember something—how to remind oneself. How to re-create one's own mind.

A book that will help me remember my children.

It is difficult to pare the content of one's book to a readable size when one is writing about the astonishing porousness that mothering has created in her every dimension, and at all scales of her selfhood—as well as the infinite junctures of that porousness with public and private violences.

It is difficult to imagine saying anything at all when it's impossible to know what one is looking at, anymore—when information's smoke and mirrors are arranged so as to disallow clear understanding of what one is looking at, anymore.

It is difficult to create a book's arc when one is meditating about things that lie beyond the scale of unassisted human perception—a single microbe as the structural center around which a snowflake forms.

And geological time's loss of winter on earth as a result of human-induced climate change, I.

It is difficult to assemble all of this together within an affective cultural shift that I will attempt, across this book, to metonymize via the government's destruction of the brains of whales with sonar. I

I haven't *written this book*, I've gathered fragments across a few thousand mornings during which my body and brains felt susceptible.

During which my body and brains succumbed to. Years of astonishing porousness, during which I have wondered: do I have a soul.

Do I have a mind. Is this *love* that is dissolving me. And is my soul

actually the raw nerve of some great wealth. Is my soul the bomb that landed

at the center of my torso, exploding—the sternum of this book.

This book that has sputtered out of the holes, across many years, during which I was interrupted every few seconds, I.

Good morning love. Come here.

Winter

Oskar is curled up in my arms in front of the fire, right now—his board books are scattered all around us. I'd wanted to be here alone, to have no body on top of me, to have no body inside of me, to have only my own mind and within that mind—the long, coherent thought that I—but Oskar often wakes, even from the deepest sleep, the moment I consider leaving the bed.

I often say to my students: what are you *not* writing about in your poem?

I say things like: what is left out of the poem is just as important as what's inside of the poem.

I say: is this poem functioning as a closed or an open-system matrix?

But when I am alone at my desk by the window in the middle of the night with a cup of coffee, and when I'm fractured or liquified, and trying to gather up my.

And when I'm worrying,

I ask myself things like: what is the difference between porousness—and transcendence?

Between susceptibility—and transcendence.

What is the difference between loving someone more than oneself—and transcendence.

What is the difference between the depths or limitations of human kindness—and disassociation.

I just want to know how to ruin systems that are fundamentally invisible.

Winter

There is exquisite tenderness and an astonishing noise in this home. And this home is in a beautiful place. There is insidiousness all around us—I try to place it, I.

A few years later: Trying to arrange this book, I've found many fragments almost identical to the fragment above. I wrote these fragments wherever I was—on the peninsula, in Montana, in Arizona, in California, in Cambodia, in Vietnam, in the Ivory Coast.

Right now it is winter and we are living again in Phoenix. Archie is sitting in front of the space heater next to me singing a song to the space heater. It's about ducks—but he's fucking with me. He's really saying "fuck," and he knows I can't hear very well, so every time I lean close to him to hear the word he laughs and changes it back to duck.

And it makes me wonder—has this been a book, for all this time, about trying to hear. About straining to perceive. And all of the limitations I.

Winter

We're at my parents' house in Montana. There is both an exquisite tenderness and an astonishing noise in this house.

This house is in a beautiful place, but there's an insidiousness all around us—I try to place it. My dad is dying.

It is snowing. It is nighttime. I'm the only one awake. Snow is falling on the evergreens outside.

I made a fire—it is filling the room with flickering orange light. Oskar, Mateo and Archie are cuddled up in my childhood bedroom down the hall. In that room the wooden shelves hold plastic horses, a trophy, some photos and books. The bed is my same bed.

I can't remember how old I am when I'm alone in this house at night. When I'm in this flickering light.

Sometimes I catch myself looking at this room—fireplace, wooden ceiling, Christmas tree in the corner—with the mind of my twelve-year-old self. I was once twelve years old in this room. I was once seven years old in this room. Staring at the fire, my mind shifts through many of the minds it has been in this room.

I have been so many of my selves in this room, and now my children have also.

My dad is dying of congestive heart failure down the hall. The snow is falling all around us—all of us, right now, are inside of the same house—and it is *this* house. This house that holds far ends of my memory—my children, my parents, I.

All of us, right now—inside this house—we are alive.

Christmas Eve

My dad will try to have the final heart surgery of his life in February, but it won't happen. Instead, he will die. I have just finished putting out the children's gifts from Santa and filled everyone's stockings.

I was once the child waiting for Christmas, in the same bed that my three children are sleeping in, right now.

I was once the child staring at this Christmas tree—I am trying to keep the layers of time straight—how old I am, who I am, right now.

I have sometimes tried to describe my mind, in the months and years after the births and the breastfeeding of my children, as having experienced a kind of important damage. I—too soon, they're awake.

Winter

I have sometimes tried to describe my mind, in the months and years after the births and the breastfeeding of my children, as having experienced a kind of brain damage.

But I don't mean *brain damage* in a pejorative or a funny or a damning sense—I mean a kind of *important human damage.*

A crucial damage that happens to some humans.

I mean damage in the way that adolescence can feel like damage— when our human brains break, and then change.

I mean damage like the moments after each of us is born must feel like damage—when our human brains break, and then change.

I mean that in these years of pregnancy, giving birth, breastfeeding, and taking care of my young children, I have felt occur in my brains an important human damage—

damage that has enabled me, or forced me, to transform from one kind of human into another—

to transform into their mother, maybe. Transform into paradox, incarnate—which opens up, inside of me, into.

The ways in which some kinds of damage can become beautiful, and some cannot. This sparkling Christmas tree is so beautiful. Snow is falling in the window behind it.

I've taken out so many of the interruptions. I've tried to replace some coherence: I was once the child in this room.

And she is here again, right now.

Winter

Now Oskar is drawing pirate ships and trying to read. Now Oskar is writing his own books. Now Mateo is writing books, too. Now Archie is writing his first word, and it is "EMPIR."

Time, I.   If I try to sort out time.

If I try to put this book into some kind of order from its thousands of scraps of paper.

If I try to understand *place* and *time* within these layers of smashed-together brains in the family-animal, these conglomerated minds and bodies of the family-animal—

these layered places, and these layered memories, this sternum I.

Winter

Morning, pitch black, rain, no fire, coffee.

Time to write something eternal. Time to write something universal: I am pregnant again, right now. If this one lasts, it will be my second living baby.

Oskar is one and a half. He's upstairs, asleep in his father's arms. They are warm. It's very cold down here.

A paradox appeared inside of me the moment I became pregnant for the first time:

first, this cluster of cells is something that I think of as *my child;* second, I've never been more certain that women should have the ability to abort.

I have had the thought, since my first pregnancy, that if men get war, then I get abortion.

I have had the thought: *not wanting this* is ancient—billions of women throughout human time have *not wanted this.*

The pregnancy thrills each time, the miscarriage brings relief each time—is this something eternal.

Is this something universal. Clarice Lispector said Death takes place in my very being—how can I explain it to you.

Is this poetic. Does this have anything to do with winter.

Winter

It is *pouring, pouring, pouring* rain. We are out of coffee so I've made green tea. So much anxiety this morning I.

During these years of babies—I have felt *extreme susceptibility*, and *porousness.*

I have felt sensations and information, originating from somewhere outside of me, now very easily enter my fields of selfhood.

Sometimes the sensations emanate from the babies—allowing me to receive direct information from them, to better keep them alive.

I've begun to refer to our conglomeration of brains and bodies inside this cabin as the *family-animal*—we are exactly the same, we are never separate, and we are completely different from each other.

Sensations enter the psyche of the family-animal from networks of living things that I haven't been closely attuned to since my childhood—trees. Fungal mats. Mold. The microbes at centers of snowflakes.

And the pinging from the naval and industrial sonar surrounding this peninsula is exploding not just the brains of whales and other sea creatures—it is also directly entering and exploding the brains of our family-animal, I.

There is something I want to do in a poem like scream.

Or gasp. Or choke. Or cower. Or flail. Or moan.

If I could make a poem that is the same noise as the silence at the end of a sob—I am bent over, my mouth is open, I can neither inhale nor exhale—a poem that is the silent suspension at the end of a sob, I—.

A poem that is spent, is aghast.

If I could make a poem about winter that screams the scream of proliferating extinctions—

that scream sounds exactly like the brains of whales draining out of
their ears,

and into these waters, around us.

Winter

This valley shocks me with its living-ness. The living-ness of the Montana valley where I grew up was quieter, subtler—a deep rumble of living all around my childhood.

Here, the living and the dying occurs at all scales and pitches. The Skokomish Valley is filled with water, farming, salmon, eagles, a herd of elk with a fourteen-day route that brings them, every two weeks, to our back pasture for a night and a long morning. The river flows down from the foothills of the Olympic Mountains behind us—what people here simply call "the Olympics." There are also river-sized creeks and small creeks and streams and permanent waterfalls deeper into the mountains around us, and spontaneous waterfalls that appear very close to our home during the heavy rains.

The Skokomish River empties into the estuary, where the freshwater of the river meets the seawater in the fjord. When the tide rises in the fjord, the mouth of the river is inundated with the incoming tide and, especially during the months of rains, the river floods the valley.

Depending upon whether the valley is completely flooded or not, we can time our drives into and out of the valley, to and from our home, by looking at the tide schedule.

The valley is flooding right now. We are far-enough back that the waters have never yet made it to our property. They have always stopped a few hundred yards away.

I can't see anything. It's still too dark. The rain is falling.

Since we moved into this cabin on the peninsula, almost two years ago, I have been waking up before anyone else. At three or four or five in the morning. With the single goal of writing a poem about winter.

By which I mean I just want to try to recover something of the mind that I used to have. By which I mean I want to recover the ability to have a sustained thought without being interrupted every few seconds by a baby who.

By which I mean I want to reduce the number things entering and glutting and then pouring back out of my brains, especially my most primitive reptilian brains stimulated by danger.

By which I mean I want to quiet something.

I want to still something. I want to recover something. I want to ignite something of my old interior—something that is *only myself*—not something emanating from somewhere outside of me, or emanating from something not-me inside of me, or emanating from something that is latched onto me.

By which I mean that the extreme porousness I've experienced since the birth of Oskar, it is—.

The goal—to wake early and write a single poem about winter— continues for several years. Not just in wintertime but all year round, and then even after Mateo is born, and then even after Archie is born.

It continues during all the years we live on the peninsula, and then all during the years after that when we live in Los Angeles while we do our PhD's, and then in the Ivory Coast where we live during Todd's Fulbright fellowship and by my own research grant.

I will try to wake up before the children, and I will try to write a poem, about winter—as a clearing.

As a reckoning. As a meditation. As a silencing. As a provoking. As a stopping. As a knowing. As an elegy for winter.

As a devotion. As an effulgence. As a memory-keeping. As an attempt to see something clearly. As a practice, and desperation—

it's not that my life is difficult or beautiful, it's that children are being blown up somewhere, right now.

Winter

And what can I—

if something besides humans controlled humans—like the weather.
Like the tides. Like system collapses.

It is our second winter on the peninsula. I still cannot believe how
much it rains and snows here, though I shouldn't be surprised—we
live in a temperate rainforest.

Oskar is two years old. It is very early—maybe two or three in the
morning. He woke with me in the pitch dark and wanted to go outside.

He's out there right now, wandering around in the snowy garden while
I watch him from the window. I can barely see him in the blackness—

snow is falling on him right now.

I've now written a couple journals filled with these abandoned or
scattered bits of winter poems, in these dark hours of morning.

In the winter poems, I'm usually staring out the window, like this,
watching the snow or the rain—

many of them just a few words before I. Like right now. He's pounding
on the door, right now.

Excruciatingly tender explosion, I.

Winter

It's November. Salmon are filling the creek a few feet away from this desk. They are spawning, and they are so thick and loud that even I, mostly deaf, can hear them thrashing if I have my hearing aids in.

They're outside my window, right now.

The salmon are two or three feet long, and the creek is about five feet across. The water appears to be made entirely of salmon.

Right here—Todd explained to Oskar, as they squatted by the edge of the creek, as Oskar reached down with one still-fat baby finger to barely touch the back of a spawning salmon—right here is the spot to which the salmon have *unendingly returned.*

I am filled with such—when I hear them thrashing from my desk.

This pencil in my hand, this baby nursing in my arms, I—.

Every year around this time the local television news shows the salmon zipping or slapping across the Skokomish Valley Road during the high-tide floodwater that crests twice a day. The Skokomish Valley Road is the single road that runs roughly parallel to the river, and down the length of the valley.

The river's route and depths and behaviors have altered significantly in living memory because of the Cushman Hydroelectric Project, which built two large dams in the mountains behind our home. And because of the dirt runoff caused by decades of extensive logging.

No matter how many times I have tried to trace the maps on this computer screen—the creeks, the rivers, the roads—I still can't understand what exactly flows into what, what crosses what, what corresponds with the reasons why the salmon still try to swim their more-ancient route which now crosses through fields, and the road on which we drive to and from our home.

I want to say, once they reach the road, that most of the salmon make it back again to the river—though several get stranded each time the tide flows back out into the estuary, and they have to wait, panting on the wet road and in the soggy fields, for the next high tide to arrive in a few hours. Each round the eagles feast on some of them.

Like other residents of the valley we often stop our car to move the still-living salmon off the road while they wait for the next high tide.

People from surrounding areas drive over to the valley during the salmon run to record videos of the fish crossing the road.

Some open the trunks of their cars and throw a few of the stranded fish in.

From the perch of his carseat Oskar is devastated to see the stranded fish.

He's devastated to see the living fish thrown into the trunks of cars.

He's devastated that the fish don't simply stay in the river, and instead fling themselves across the fields—the new bend of it inconsistent with what they are sure they know of the river.

Winter

It is my birthday and Thanksgiving this week. My parents are visiting—they're asleep upstairs in the second bedroom that no one ever sleeps in. Oskar and Todd are asleep, as well.

It is very early in the morning. It is snowing. I am eight and a half months pregnant. I am teaching several classes at the local community college. I recently qualified for health insurance. I vehemently do not want to transcend.

I do not want to leave this moment in time. I want to—it's so hard to focus, I.

I want to be exactly here—he's awake. Excruciatingly beautiful, Todd carries Oskar down the stairs and sets him in my arms. Now Todd is going back upstairs to sleep. Oskar is in my arms—how does he wake so calm.

So infinitely peaceful. Oskar is rubbing my chin and cheeks, like he always does. He is burrowing back into my body, he is relaxing back in my arms, he is staring up into my soulface, right now, I—

love made a body, for his complete mind.

Mateo is a salmon, deep inside me—and he is thrashing.

Winter

Mateo is born in a blizzard, a few days after Christmas.

During his birth I hallucinate that each of my legs is a line of mountains forming either side of this valley.

Pubic hair grows all over my body—covering me like an animal except for a few shaved square patches, like the square patches of clearcut forest all over these mountains.

My veins are the logging roads and Mateo is the river—he is flowing out of me.

Then Mateo was the river *being pulled* out of the hole they'd just cut across my abdomen. They were pulling the river, and the suction sensation and the sucking noises as they pulled the river out of me—

the sensation that they were pulling something enormous, from out from my deepest center, I—.

And some kind of animal, the whole time—it was *moaning all around me.*

Winter

Weeks have passed since I've tried to write about winter. The birth of Mateo turned, and is still turning me, inside-out.

Tonight, sitting in front of the fire, things flowing into and out of my shot-through brains, breastfeeding this beautiful new baby in my arms—my torso—my brains—my vagina and anus and bowels and bladder—they're wobbling or falling, and.

I am newly eviscerated, newly cracked-open.

The firelight flickers through this tiny baby's eyelashes, creating shadows across his face so that his face looks cracked open.

Cracked open at the sternum, and cracked open at the brains,—I.

Something of *soul* has increased, as my porousness has increased.

Something of me has diminished.

Winter

It is snowing. Mateo is sleeping tied to my chest. Oskar is sleeping in his father's arms upstairs. Mateo is so new that I feel like his soul is still somewhere inside of me.

There is a paradoxical isolation that occurs in being so populated with things that are emanating from outside of oneself.

As there is a paradoxical isolation that occurs when one is stuffed with things that are emanating from inside of oneself.

I am so full.

I am so porous.

I am so surrounded, I am so ethereal, I am so hevel, I am so sticky, I am so much the same as these babies, I am so much the same as this cabin, I am so much the same as this rug, I am so much the same as this fire, I am so much the same as this whale, I am so much the same as this sonar, I am so much the same as this nation state, I am so much the same as this bomb I.

Am I supposed to have an arc to this book—what is the shape of this book—a full circle.

A parabola. The shape, if I could create this with a computer screen or paper—is the shape of explosion.

Winter

The fire is burning very hot. This living room is so hot that I'm not wearing a shirt. Today was a quiet, beautiful day. Gray. Overcast. Dark all day long—no rain, so it felt—extremely quiet. I should be grading papers right now,

but instead I am holding this beautiful baby. The journal is resting on his butt. When Mateo sleeps he grins, and both his dimples deepen.

Mateo, oh—most peaceful—I hold you absolutely new. You're in my arms, and I—.

How does a baby— *appear*—from inside of oneself—I.

Oskar is two years old when Mateo is born in a blizzard at the very end of December. That is how we always say it:

Mateo was born in a blizzard.

I have been adjunct-teaching maximally all fall semester to maintain my health insurance until he is born and I hope I can vaginally birth him even though his older brother was born via c-section because I need to begin teaching January 4 in order to maintain our partial health insurance after he is born. But almost two weeks after his due-date I notice the baby has stopped moving so, after we throw all the food from our refrigerator and freezer out into the snow so it will keep because the electricity has gone out because the snow downed a power line somewhere in the valley, we drive to the emergency room in Olympia.

When we arrive at the emergency room they say we have to take him out right now, so I quickly have another c-section and he is born.

A few days later we find out he has contracted a MRSA infection during our three day stay at the hospital and, because I have just been cut in half in order for him to be born, I am at risk for contracting the MRSA infection from him, so we have to keep a "sterile home" while I return to adjunct teaching on January 4th in order to maintain our health insurance.

Cut in half from the c-section, taking care of the new baby with MRSA, I am adjunct teaching, and I am also taking care of the older baby whose heart is breaking because of this new baby that I.

Oskar's heart is breaking because, often—*this new baby, instead of him.*

And I am keeping a sterile home which means changing diapers with surgical masks and plastic surgical gloves, on a towel which we then wash in hot water and bleach. No visitors, I—.

> The older baby screeches for a long time because his banana broke—
>
> imagine if our invisible warfare was screeched like a baby's screech into our center-brains,
>
> imagine wifi and sonar screamed into our center-brains like that baby's screech while,
>
> my god, this tiny new baby! he is so beautiful, I—

my student evaluations for this semester will be terrible.

And therefore I will not be offered any summer classes while I receive unpaid "mentoring" through an online module that I must complete before I am offered more adjunct classes in the fall.

But this small break in teaching will disqualify us from health insurance until I've consecutively taught another two semesters. I

Winter

Coffee. Quiet. Darkness.

It was difficult to leave them this morning—Oskar holding his soft baby animals, little metal cars scattered around the bed, tiny new Mateo, and Todd—all curled up together in bed. Warm and smelling perfect, I.

Focus.

Winter   ·

This winter poem was supposed to have been a simple challenge—
write a poem about winter.

I'd do it for a few days until my writing juices were flowing again.

It was time to get my old brains back, I thought. I started when we
moved to the peninsula—Oskar had just turned one.

Right now Oskar is twelve and we are again living in Phoenix. I am
arranging this book, and I can't keep time straight.

I fall back and forth in time. I can't remember how old I am. How old
any of us are. Sometimes when I hear Oskar's voice say mama and I
turn to look at him, it's another version of Oskar I believe I'm going
to see—then there he is. Next to me right now, writing his own book.
Twelve years old.

His left hand—now as then—is full of lego guys.

The winter poem exercise was supposed to have been a generous
gesture toward myself: I love winter! And we were, at that moment,
living in a beautiful place during winter time.

Winter is a classic poetic subject—winter *lends itself* to poetry.

We had a fire and a hearth—and it's well known that fires and hearths
intensify the beauty of winter.

We had a beautiful rug in front of the fireplace! Very often there was
something baking! Very often the astonishing *wonderfulness of snow*
was falling just outside our window!

I should easily have been able to meditate upon winter, and then write
a poem about winter, I thought—

but that first winter we lived in the cabin is also the winter I began
disintegrating or dissipating into the family-animal.

And the psychic depth-charges of our nation's invisible wars began exploding my brains.

And the pinging of the naval and industrial sonar in all the waters around our peninsula began exploding my brains.

And the babies began leaking, and breaking, into any coherence I.

When the long rains and snows began in the rainforest that first winter, we were so happy. Oskar, so tiny and sweet. The cabin, so cozy. Then the next winter. Mateo is so tiny and sweet. The cabin is so cozy.

Arranging the book, years later, I keep finding pieces of paper like this:

Winter Poem:

We are so happy, I.

Winter

We are so happy.

I—*Time*.

Winter

This morning there is no fire. The rain is falling. I've opened the windows so I can better hear it.

I've been astonished by the downpours of rain that began in October and continue until, in early December, the rains were so heavy that stretches of I-5 from Portland to Seattle closed, and the coast from Oregon to British Columbia received hurricane-force gusts.

Before Christmas, the valley floods all the way from its mouth—where the Skokomish River drains into the Salish Sea—up to just a few yards from our cabin, seven miles away at the back of the valley.

During this flooding, which happens several times a year, most people who live in the valley are stuck in their homes. But we are always able to drive the logging roads through the mountains behind the house, and into the nearest small town. It can take half the day to get there, but we always have an escape route.

However, on the escape route, there is a long stretch where we have to drive the water-covered logging road as it runs alongside the flooding river—which is, right now, extremely high, extremely fast, and filled with fallen trees.

It feels sickeningly like we are driving down the edge of the river itself—as if our tires have lost their grip on the road and we're going in, the babies asleep in the backseat.

I am wrapped in a blanket while I stare out the window into this dark morning. I imagine our private property.

I imagine this shelter around me—a small cabin made of wood in the middle of the woods. The salmon are thrashing in the tributary creek, just a few feet away from my window—I can hear them. I can hear and smell the rain, and the fungal mat below the forest.

The creek, right now, looks burst-alive with the wriggling bodies of adult salmon in the black-silver water. The salmon have returned to the exact spot of their collective memory—

and that exact spot is just a few feet away from me as I write this.

I am overwhelmed with the idea of an *exact spot*. I am overwhelmed with the idea of a *most ancient home*—and of a *lifetime's accomplishment*.

I try to imagine the genetic moment, and the echo chambers of salmon memory.

Soon they will all die. Their bodies will decay, and become the soft dirt in the bed of the creek.

What I mean to say is that this world—it is a beautiful world. And:

Am I inside of this world, or am I outside of this world *boom boom*.

Boom boom noises from overhead—he's waking, and playing with his door—I.

Sometimes, on these mornings when I am alone for even a few minutes, I can feel my own mind again. When I have too much information. When too many noises and voices I.

Am I living in this world, and in this world—is there is no place outside of this world.

Am I the same thing as whatever there is.

Am I utterly unable to imagine that—clearly, or utterly—he's awake.

Winter, a few days before Christmas, twelve years later

Boom boom noises from down the hall—he's awake and playing with the door—another is awake is screaming pancakes. I am trying to revise and organize these pieces—it's 5 am in Phoenix and Archie walks into my bedroom, his wild hair sticking up everywhere. He says "I have to poop" so I point at the bathroom door. A few seconds later Mateo, still dreamy and cuddly, crawls into my bed and says "mama Archie will need you to wipe his butt in a moment." Mateo is cuddling into me right now, my right arm is wrapped around him, and his head is resting on my belly as I type. He's so gentle and warm I. Now Archie is screaming wipe my butt.

Unerringly, unceasingly, across the years—the children appear each morning, so alive, and so tender, inside of their bodies.

Their beautiful bodies—always working.

Mateo's eyes are closed and he is peaceful. He's cuddling right back into my body, just as he has always done, since the moment he was born. Even as a newborn sleeping next to me at night, I had the sensation that someone behind Mateo was pushing him hard into my belly—such was the force of his own burrowing. He's nine years old. His hands are filled with Star Wars lego guys—tiny guns are poking out between his fingers.

I imagine myself buying all my guns legally, in the middle of whatever this is, I.

Winter

Skokomish is a Twana word that means means *people of the river.* The Skokomish Reservation is at the other end of this valley, along the estuary.

I try again to trace the logging roads, to trace the water's new and ancient pathways, to trace the borders of the reservation, to trace the lines around this private property I.

I superimpose and adjust my memories and beliefs over the maps on my screen, lit by the electricity that—lines extending out from my brains.

The brains of the family-animal—all of our arteries extending outward from our bodies—down the valley, and through the electrical lines that we.

It has been difficult at times to feel myself a solid-enough, singular-enough living presence to stop writing this book which, at so many points along the way, could have been a completely different book to offer.

This book is several books, each written into each other, and destroying each other over time.

If you include all the miscarriages and the three living children and all the microbes and bacteria and yeasts inside of me,

I have been a multiverse of living and dying entities, in a cabin for a few years, in an apartment for a few years, in a house for a few years— in the middle of whatever this is.

What is making this book, I.

Roland Barthes wrote "I always behave—I insist upon behaving, whatever I am told and whatever my own discouragements may be, as if love might someday be fulfilled, as if the Sovereign Good were possible."

But it feels to me like we are killing someone right now.

Like they're killing someone for my protection. Like they are safely destroying someone while they are speaking to each other about the bright and otherworldly—while garbage all around this world is flipping or spinning right now—and writing this brings no relief.

We are living in this cabin in the forest drinking glasses of water with blood in it and looking at each other as if to say—

what should we do?

I dreamed last night that the pipes below our home were bleeding, were oozing blood into our water.

I dreamed that the pipes below our cabin were our own rotting veins, extending into the walls and floors and ceilings of the cabin from various places on all of our bodies, and so we could never again leave the cabin.

I dreamed that the walls of this cabin were the rotting corpses of trees. As if our water supply. As if our distressed conditions.

I came to this place to find goodness. I feel—get into my arms my love—as if I have.

Sovereign Good

It is three o'clock in the morning, the children are asleep. I have the most beautiful cup of coffee in my hands—it is hot, it is very strong, there is a little bit of cream in it. I am looking out the window behind my desk. I am about to have a thought. It's a coherent thought. From a complete mind, I:

> Do I love going beyond what I know.

> Do I love looking closely at something I don't understand, until it has changed me.

> Do I love looking closely at something invisible, until it has changed me.

Lorca said but hurry, let's entwine ourselves as one, our mouth broken, our soul bitten by love, so time discovers us safely destroyed.

But Fanny Howe said my brain is a baby, I.

Winter

Across the years since we bought the cabin I have arranged and rearranged this book into many formats—sometimes this has been a book of lyric poetry. Sometimes this book has been a list of questions, sometimes a collection of deeply-disrupted aphorisms. Sometimes lyric essays. Sometimes it joined with other research and writing while I completed coursework and two dissertations for my PhD. Sometimes I deleted everything and started over with lists and bullet points, then pasted everything back in again so that I could slam my head against it for a few more years.

Sometimes the materials gathered for this book have been a thousand pages long—the scattered writings of all those mornings, gathered together.

And once I deleted and deleted until the words barely gasped themselves out onto each page, a pool of white around them. Pieces of this book have been pulled out of emails, then deleted from the book again. I've used portions of letters, journals, and checked my memory against news sites on the internet.

As the world changes, the book has to change. As my children have been born and have changed, the book has to change. As my brains have dissolved into the brains of the family-animal, into the whale, into the forest, into the fungal mat—the book has to change.

Sometimes I try to write down these morning desperations, these morning weather reports—from inside of our deepest-tendernesses.

I want to write from within our deepest-kindness, we.

I am writing forth from the entrails of our family-animal—

I want to extend our tentacles toward whatever are the origins of the naval and industrial pinging—deep in those waters all around us—in order to destroy them.

I am amazed when the babies speak words I've never heard before,

but long to understand.

Winter

At the edge of the kitchen is the only stairway in our home—it is steep, and like everything else in the cabin it was handmade by the people who lived here before us. The stairs go up for twelves steps, turn 180 degrees at the landing, then go up another eight steps. The stairs themselves are made of thick, polished wood boards that have been nailed to parallel beams angled upward, with about ten inches of open space between each board. If one of our children were to slip as they ascended or descended the stairs, and if their feet fell through the space between the boards, their bodies would follow through easily but their heads would not fit—they would dangle there, stuck below the chin and the base of their skulls, until their necks snapped and they were dead.

Winter

It's sometime in the second or third year of this project and I've begun to think of the winter poem not as a poem, but as an attempt to focus on something crucial—it is not a poem, but a *reminding*.

When I try to write the poem about winter, I am trying to hold, tenderly, onto something of the childhoods of my children—my children are flowing right past me, and into the world.

The winter poem has become a lament about time, a lament for winter.

It's a lament for everything, and praise.

An act of worry. Or anxiety, I.

I begin to think of the winter poem not as a poem, but as a devotion.

I began to think of the winter poem not as a poem, but as a test of my soul.

Or proof of my selfhood—

do I have these things, and have I ever had them.

I—he's awake. He's coming down the stairs, right now.

Winter

Don't.

Don't.

But I love your face mama thank you you're welcome.

And not in my nose either, love, or my eyes, or my buttons.

Don't.

Winter

He screams for a long time on the floor next to me while I write
something about winter. I bend over, to pick up the screaming baby.

I am bending over.

I am spreading my butt cheeks as far apart as I can to reveal
something, I.

I am lifting him, toward my face. He screams into my face—

he screams the emergency, he screams the noise and the speed at
which the noise—

noise directly into my brains' most-center

until I am forced to understand *center* differently. I

Winter

For a couple years now I've tried to describe this book to people who ask me what I'm working on, and I have never felt that I could: It's a book about the loss of winter because of climate change, because of ocean acidification I.

It's a book about the important dissolution of the mind as I've experienced it during these years of pregnancy, breast-feeding, and taking care of very young children—and the resultant wisdom I. During which time I have been deeply and completely interrupted every few seconds, for years on end. It's a book about the loss of coherence—it's a book about *another kind of coherence*, I.

It's a book about trying to write while one's mind is exploded by utter love, and also by military and industrial sonar.

It's a book in which the fevers of the children echo the heating of the earth.

It's a book about making new life during the sixth wave of mass extinctions.

It's a book that wants to say: though there is love—we are waging an invisible war.

It's a book that wants to say: though this baby is excruciatingly tender—so are the babies beneath our bombs excruciatingly tender.

I'm re-writing Ecclesiastes. I'm re-writing Proverbs. I'm revising Modernism. I'm—

with certainty, I have thought of this book as a Wisdom Literature— and my imperfect longing for more wisdom literature written by anyone who cares about something else more than they care about themselves.

It's a book about my father dying then Trump being elected. And in the middle of that: sons.

It's a book to help me discriminate between revelation and noise—the internet, the pinging, the children.

I have thought of the book as a diary, or as a daybook, or as a way of holding together the pieces of what used to be myself—my *self* before they were born, I.

I have thought of this book as a way of holding onto the excruciating preciousness of my children.

A book to hold the love that is, right now, exploding all of us in this cabin.

It's a book about an idea of *self* that is very old, or perhaps very new.

It's a book about learning to be their mother, by which I mean—it's a book about learning how to rip open my own heart to love this world so much that—it becomes a book about enemies.

And paranoia. And anxiety.

This book is a meditation on the ethics of killing my enemies.

Because when the babies left my body and were placed in my arms, I saw the passion of the assemblages that they had just been made from. From the first moment I saw my babies, I understood that the assemblages were constructed of fragility,

and that the world has an instinct for devouring fragility.

When the babies arrived I began to devise the killing of my enemies:

executives at chemical companies oil companies pipeline lobbyists all mining companies all billionaires packs of dogs Monsanto and anyone who makes the precariousness not stop—

when my first baby arrived I began to beg.

I sharpened my teeth I fell to my knees.

I thought about "what you did not do for the least ones you did not do for me" and began to—I didn't sleep. I began to ask what is "the least one," what is "the most one," and what is this sweetness at the core of my rage, I.

I didn't wake. And I never *truly slept* I.

When the first baby arrived, at the very moment he was placed in my arms—I imagined bending over.

Reaching back to spread my butt cheeks as far apart as I could, to show you something I.

Practically begging my soul to reveal itself.

I wanted to open, open at the center part I.

I wanted to crack open, wherever I felt such pressure, and I—

it is a book about about catholicism. It's a catholic book.

It's a book in which a catholic imagination meets the sixth wave of mass extinction—I'm drinking some very exquisite coffee.

I am all alone, for at least a few minutes, it is snowing hard in the darkness—I am so happy.

The coherence of my cup of coffee.

And the coherence of the sleep of my children, asleep in the arms of their father. I

Winter

Mateo and Oskar don't know the word gun and call them *boom-booms* instead. I don't know when they saw their first gun—it would have been on television, or in a book, or in one of their lego sets.

Todd's dad is a Vietnam vet on full disability for PTSD. He comes to our home several times a week in his camouflage pants, t-shirt, and baseball cap to chop wood for us, or bring us a salmon he's smoked, or jam that Lindy has made from berries he picked in the woods around our cabin, and always to throw Oskar up into the air, his head so close to the low wooden ceiling of the cabin that I can see his brains smashed there—smashed all over the ceiling—over and over and over—while they both laugh so hard.

And I say, or I scream, over and over: Don't.

Don't. Don't.

Winter

Mateo, are you a fish? No.
Mateo are you the moon? No.
Mateo are you pink? No. (He is.)
Mateo are you hugging me? No. (He is.)
Mateo are you a tree? No.
Mateo are you a baby? No. (He is.)
Mateo are drones killing someone right now? No. (They are.)
Mateo do you like cookies? No. (Now he is shoving his mouth full
of cookies.)
Mateo are you cuddling with me? No. (He is.)
Mateo are you clutching at me desperately? No. (He is.)
Mateo are you bereft because your cookies are all gone? No. (He is.)
Mateo are you saying no or snow? No. (He is.)

Winter

We are alive in a beautiful place.

The ocean is a few minutes away, and for three seasons of the year
the Skokomish River and its tributary creeks will regularly flood this
valley, keeping us here for days at a time.

Right now the floodwaters have risen to fill the valley, stopping a short
walk away from our property.

Right now there is a fire in the fireplace, and the dark wooden interior
of the cabin is even darker than usual. Right now they are sleeping
upstairs while the rain makes a dull roar all around me.

Later today we will drive out of the valley on logging roads, over the
mountains behind us on narrow, rugged roads that are dark even
during the daytime—dark from the forest canopy and from the cloud
cover during the rainy seasons.

We will pass spontaneous waterfalls, pouring down the steep slopes
and covering the road. We will drive through the runoff from the
waterfalls, we will drive over a bridge made for logging trucks. It's a
labyrinthine trip, and over the years we memorize all the turns and
forks until we feel comfortable on the signless, wet roads. In the dark,
with food, water, blankets, the chainsaw, and extra fuel in the trunk.

I love this long trip into town. I love the interference of weather and
water into our daily lives. I love our susceptibility to what is happening
around us on earth.

To live in this valley on the peninsula feels both like we are living at
the top of the mountains and at the bottom of the sea—

there is a child standing quietly at the top of the stairs, right now.

He is looking down at me. He is looking down at his mother, who is
writing by the fireplace. She looks out the window over her desk and
sees him, reflected there, standing at the top of the stairs. He wonders
if something is baking.

A cold up of coffee sits in front of her. She.

Winter

I've been teaching night classes at the local community college—a tiny campus that looks like a ranger station in a national park. Two other women teach composition classes there, and we are becoming friends. Todd is teaching farther away at another community college. In order to qualify for health insurance, you have to teach full-time for two consecutive semesters. An unofficial policy has emerged, during what we are now calling *the recession*, to slightly reduce an adjunct's teaching load every other semester in order to disqualify them from receiving health insurance.

Sometimes we have classes, sometimes we have health insurance.

The mind of the family-animal pulsing *do you have to poop?*

I can't actually write if you're touching me.

Winter

Mama *ho-me ho-me ho-me ho-me ho-me*!

Mama *ho-me ho-me ho-me ho-me ho-me*!

Mama *ho-me ho-me ho-me ho-me ho-me*!

Mama *ho-me ho-me ho-me ho-me ho-me*!

Mama *ho-me ho-me ho-me ho-me ho-me*!

Mama *ho-me ho-me ho-me ho-me ho-me*!

Mateo, I *am* holding you.

Winter

Oskar's woken with me this morning. I have a cup of coffee. He has a
cup of cocoa.

My job is to transcribe.

I fight bad guy skeletons, he says. I fight creatures that eat people
I can do that myself. Do you know how I do it? I pick up big sticks
they are so big and then I throw them at them. And they start to die.

I fight meat-eater skeletons. I fight eagle skeletons. I don't fight
plant-eater skeletons because plant-eaters are nice. I read him what I
have written, and he says

I want you to add "My love." My love, I usually don't want to be eaten.
I really don't like to be eaten by ghosts, my love, because then I
would die.

Do you know why ghosts eat people?

Because ghosts are really strong. If you get eaten, then you die. My love.

Winter

I am losing language as my children are gaining theirs.

I am losing my coherence as the children are gaining theirs.

I am losing my belief in all the systems of earth just as the children are beginning to apprehend them.

The empire wants his Dark Vader cape attached to his shirt with rubber bands.

The other empire holds my finger as he nurses. As he nurses, he stares unwaveringly into my soulface.

While the other empire floats inside me. Another head, floating somewhere inside of me.

Baby: shameless! Shameless!

Did he say shameless?

Winter

It is so cold down here this morning. The kitchen's disgusting.

I am at the limits of my saying. These scraps of repetitive coherences and incoherences are.

I can try to say how both the light and the darkness that are inside of me pour out into the babies when they suck me into themselves.

As the babies suck me into themselves, they gaze into my cracked-open soulface.

What am I doing down here every morning. Am I tracking the losses of the smallest and largest pieces of my human portions of time—simultaneous with my infinite small and large human joys—

this perfect moment happened, and it is already gone.

Right after the babies are born, some most-center part of me liquifies, or is torn.

And the susceptibility, tearing I.

48 women are raped every hour in the Congo during war time, this study says.

Every 107 seconds an American woman is sexually assaulted, this study says. It doesn't count children under 12.

Am I an open-system matrix, sitting in front of this fire while holding this beautiful baby.

Or am I a closed-system matrix, sitting in front of this fire, while holding this baby. I—

Winter

A pirate's sword is not a cypress, but a cutlass.

Can you say cutlass?

Take your pacifier out and say cutlass.

Winter

Coffee. Window. Ice,

once the center-spot, behind my brain-sternum *mama* cracks, I.

Winter

No one slept last night. Both the babies are in my arms right now. Todd just checked Mateo: 103.3 and Oskar: 102.2. The journal is balanced on Oskar's shoulder. They won't sleep unless they are right on top of me and they've finally fallen asleep I.

It is flooding in the valley right now. And we don't have health insurance right now.

Winter

I've been using the word "cabin," but I worry that the word cabin conjures the romantic image of whole logs piled horizontally on top of each other to form both the inner and the outer walls of a cozy home that is situated next to a lake or a river. Just as when, in a few pages, I will first use "pig" you might imagine a smallish pink animal. The word cabin describes our home because of the building's diminutive size, its dark brown wood exterior, and its location in the middle of a forest, next to a creek. I use the word cabin because our home requires the heat from its wood burning stove to warm us during three seasons of the year, when we will receive anywhere from 100 to 140 inches of rain and, depending upon the year, several snowfalls, snowstorms, and ice storms.

This cabin is actually just a small, dark, brown house with an orange door. It doesn't seem like the kind of building someone would live in year-round, but we do.

I worry that by using the word cabin it will be believed that life inside the cabin has been cozy and peaceful, remote, and removed.

The inside of the cabin is alternately full of screaming or peaceful children.

I know that what I am about to say is less necessary at this point in the book, but I want so badly for you to know that I am I am both an open-system matrix and a closed-system matrix, sitting here by the fire.

I want you to know that there is pretty rug in front of the fire, that very often something is baking.

I am sitting in front of the fireplace wondering what I always wonder—wondering about the same things I wondered when I was a child—

who is innocent, and for how long.

What is good. What is right.

What *makes* us—and what of ourselves is our own.
What are the edges and the limitations of my responsibilities.

What is the work that will never end, I—oh here you are my love.
Come here. Get into my arms.

Let me focus:

Winter

It's twelve years later and I've just been revising the page before this one. It is very early in the morning, we are living again in Phoenix, and I've hidden myself in the bedroom to do final revisions of this book. At the exact moment when, on the previous page, the child crawls into his mother's arms while she is trying to write, the three children run into the room where I am revising and arranging.

The children want to be in this room because I am not with them, so their instinct is to find me—they are a pack of shepherding dogs with one sheep. Archie smacks the computer with the plastic knight sword left over from Mateo's Halloween costume. Archie is five years old, and now he's sticking the sword between his legs so that it extends far behind him. Now Archie says "hey Mateo look at my butt-penis" and Oskar says "Archie stop it" and Mateo laughs and grabs the sword and sticks it between his own legs the same way Archie just did, and now they are all screaming *butt-penis*. Now I'm screaming butt-penis, too.

We're all screaming butt-penis and we're laughing so hard I.

What is good. What is right.

What *makes* us—and what of ourselves is our own.

Winter

Firelight flickers over this baby's heartbreakingly-peaceful face. His sleeping mouth becomes slack around my nipple, and the milk that had collected in his cheek is flowing back out of his mouth, down his neck, onto my breast and now it's trickling down my sternum.

His eyelashes cast shadows on his cheek in the moving firelight, and the shadows resemble insects.

The firelight disrupts the shadows over his body until his legs stretch out to adult length, his torso thickens into a man's torso, his diaper becomes a cloth over his waist and the shadows from his eyelashes are now gashes and wounds on his bearded face.

His open mouth is dripping not with milk but with blood, and my child is dead.

We are both bloody, and our open mouths are screaming silently because we are deadened, and we are becoming dead—I.

We are brutal, as I hold him in my arms in front of the fireplace.

We are nothing like Michelangelo's placid marble Pietà, and we are not innocent.

I no longer wonder about innocence in the context of catholicism, I do now wonder who is innocent and for how long in the context of being a white human mother alive during late capitalism while oceans around her acidify—

and I am, at all times, both extremely confused and extremely certain.

I wonder things, as I look at this sleeping baby in my arms—no blood is dripping from his mouth, right now.

And his finger is not on a button. Nor on a trigger.

Our hands are not—right now—around any throat.

Winter

Years later, as I do final revisions on the page before, it is Christmastime again. Archie sings O holy night as I revise—he is five years old.

I am trying so hard to *mark time*. I am trying so hard, for so long, to hold something infinitely-layered inside myself.

Archie has added the phrase "googolplex-infinity" into O Holy night—I.

Mateo asks what a googolplex is, and Oskar says it's a *portmanteau*, I.

Time.

Winter

Two years after we bought the cabin I chased three pigs in a downpour while holding baby Mateo on my hip. The pigs had broken through the plywood sty that we'd nailed together, and they were trying to head for the forest. Mike was on his way to help; Todd was teaching. We'd bought the pigs as babies a few months before because we wanted to try to raise our own food, but we were also raising two small children and trying to teach and write so, although we did eventually eat the pigs, we could have done it better. They were near the end of their lives, just about to be slaughtered by our neighbor, and were probably unhappy with their living arrangement. We'd underestimated how large the pigs would grow—so even though the sty we built them seemed huge when they were babies, even with our additions it was too small now. Also, the layout of the farmyard made it impossible for the chickens to move freely between their coop and the forest—where they liked to spend their days foraging slugs—without being eaten by the pigs. So, Todd had constructed a "sky-bridge" to allow the chickens to walk over the pigs' sty and into the forest—passing just a few feet over the pigs' heads.

I believe the unequal freedoms of the animals tormented the pigs.

Something tormented the pigs. Pigs return to a feral state quickly and so, being imprisoned while the wilderness is all around them—this proximity likely tormented the pigs.

On the day I'm describing the pigs were enormous, grey, and pissed off. One of them had bitten my finger that morning while I was feeding them windfall apples. We were raising one for ourselves to eat, one for our neighbors, and one for our parents to share. The pigs were consuming all the kitchen and garden leftovers and large buckets of feed every few hours by this point, and they each easily weighed more than I did.

They were now loose in the front yard—I tried to herd them back, as I used to herd horses. But I was afraid of these pigs as I'd never been afraid of a horse.

Plus I was carrying Mateo, who must have been seven or eight months old at this point. Mateo *loved* the pigs. He also loved running around in the rain with me. He was calmly and deeply enjoying the problem. I shifted my goal—instead of getting them back into the sty, I would just try to keep the pigs out of the forest until Mike arrived.

The chickens were hiding on branches of trees at the edge of the forest, watching as Mateo and I dashed back and forth in the mud and the rain, between the pigs and the trees. I remember thinking that at any moment the pigs might as well turn and chase me—and if they did, and if I slipped, I remember thinking, I could save myself, but they'd probably eat Mateo.

That same night, breastfeeding Mateo in front of the fire, I write down this list of questions on the back of my recipe for cherry snowball cookies:

> who is in the sty, who is on the sky-bridge, who is flying into a
> sty to be eaten, who is in the cabin, who is coming to help,
> who is breaking through plywood, who is being caught, who
> is repairing the fence, who is hiding in the trees, who is
> eating the other, who is raised to be eaten, who is free to
> forage, who is enjoying the problem, who is who is blocking
> the forest, who is blocking the forest,
>
> who is blocking the forest. Who is innocent, and for
> how long.

Winter

It's dark, it's half-snowing and half-raining and I've just come back in from feeding the chickens.

After I take off my red rubber boots and hang up my raincoat, I enter what is almost the entirety of the cabin—the living room and the kitchen.

There is no wall between these rooms—just a long, golden-brown polished wood counter with no cabinets underneath. We put stools at the counter, and that is where we eat.

Almost everything in the cabin's constructed interior is brown— brown polished wood counter, brown wood floors, brown wood ceiling, wood bookshelves, wood cabinets.

Everything else that has entered the cabin since we moved in is bright and mismatched and was given to us by our families. The 1980's-era turquoise velvet sofa with large pink and yellow flowers on it—from Todd's parents' basement. A shiny gold easy chair with tiny flowers on it that belonged to Todd's grandpa. A puffy maroon recliner my parents gave me as a gift after Oskar was born, so that I could breastfeed him comfortably. A beautiful orange, red and gold rug, also a gift from my parents.

The focal point of the cabin is always either the fire or the oven, if something is baking.

The desk I am writing at is tiny—just a bit larger than this computer. Todd's grandma bought it for me at her church fundraiser—it fits perfectly between the fireplace and the bookshelf. When I sit at the desk I look out a window onto the creek. My back is to the kitchen.

Behind the kitchen is the stairway.

At the top of the stairs is a bedroom. Inside the bedroom are the children. They are sleeping, curled around their father.

When I sit at my desk each morning

I am directly below them while they sleep: I know what this looks like.

I know we look like the monsters of heteronormativity, we.

The focal point of our home right now: sparkling Christmas tree.

Christmas Eve, Phoenix, years later

My dad has been dead for five years. Archie is five and a half. Mateo will turn ten in a few days. Oskar is twelve, and he's sitting next to me right now, writing his own book—it's a piece of Philip K. Dick fan fiction. It's 4:30 in the morning. I have just a few days left to get this to my publisher. It hurts to arrange this book. It hurts to think of walking away from the binders and files and scraps and pieces of these many years of failed and accumulating winter poems. I don't remember if each one hurt to write, but of these scraps, all together—their repetitions and food stains and mind-alteringly frustrated cross-outs and interruptions on top of interruptions—their voice running over voice, running over noise—the pinging around us—only *all of this all together*—resembles, sometimes still, the insides of us, right now I.

It hurts—with tenderness, and with the profoundest frustrations I have ever felt—to look at these pieces.

It would hurt someone to read them. It hurts to think of ending these years in the form of a book, to possibly be walking away from my children's youngest years of childhood—to finish this book.

The tangle we were, now slightly untangling.

Everyone else is sleeping. I have a cup of coffee. Oskar has a cup of tea.

Todd's mom and my mom are both here for Christmas, sleeping down the hall, as are Mateo and Archie.

Todd set up a light outside that makes it look like snow is falling on the front of the house. From the corner of my eye it really appears that snow is falling outside the window.

We have turned on the gas fireplace for Christmas Eve morning—just for Oskar and me.

Oskar asks if I want to watch an X-files. Yeah, I really do.

Winter

Effulgences. Devotions.

O, the tenderness, I—.

O, my children asleep in a pile in my arms while I try to write this—
stretching my finger to press one key at a time—

does it matter.

How long does it matter—Oskar is sitting beside me drawing the
moon over a pirate ship. The moon pulls.

The moon pulls the waves up, but not the snow.

That's right love.

In order to think clearly I need something that I don't have.

Winter

I want Dark Vader on my penis.

And so I put his underwear on him backwards.

Some people like Dark Vader on their butthole.

Yes.

Mama the people who made this underwear think that most kids like Dark Vader on their butthole.

Yes, that seems true.

I like him on my penis because then I can see him if I want to.

That's a good point.

See I just bend over and look at Dark Vader.

Just like that!

Except he's upside down when I bend over to look at him on my penis.

Oskar: Yeah Mateo, that's a flaw in the design.

Winter

There is poop on Dark Vader. Yes.

Poop leaked onto Dark Vader. Yes.

Poop leaked directly from my butthole onto Dark Vader.

Yes it did.

Winter

We hardly ever leave the cabin together these days—I teach at the community college a couple of evenings a week. Todd leaves a bit more often, teaching during the day and working at a local literacy organization. The house smells like poop this morning. Poop and rain.

But other than teaching we are always here—and usually, we are all in this exact room—the wood-covered living room that fades into the wood-covered kitchen, with the forest all around us.

I love to imagine I am an animal, and this is our home in the forest, I say to Oskar. You *are* an animal and this *is* our home in the forest, mama, he says.

It's been raining so hard for so many weeks—. Later this morning I will bundle the boys up in winter jackets underneath their raincoats, and we will go gather eggs, crossing the chicken-shit filled mud in our boots.

When we come back inside, like most of our mornings, this cabin will smell like our own shit mixed with chicken shit—the boys are singing, to the tune of "Skip to My Lou": Poop, poop, poop from my butt. Poop, poop, poop from my butt. Poop from my butt my darling—we are now in what catholicism calls Ordinary Time.

If catholicism contains the maw. The butthole. The invisible war. The obscene maternal.

So much anxiety, overlaying so much claustrophobic—*rootedness*— this morning, I

Winter

If catholicism contains the maw. The butthole. The invisible war. The obscene maternal.

If the obscene maternal is a refusal of the statehood maternal.

If out of my butthole I gave birth to aporia, parables, paradox, irresolvables, the hinge, I.

Then—this morning, I am resolved—I am finally going to take a shower.

If I want to take a shower, then the children must be in the bathroom with me—playing with some toys I've placed on the floor around them.

Within a few minutes, the children will have crawled into the shower with me.

I take off their wet clothes, and we all sit naked on the floor of the shower.

We're pretending that we're outside in the rain that is actually raining on our cabin, right now—

but oh no!, wait a minute—

we forgot to put on clothes before we went outside mama! now we're in danger!

If we hold each other close we won't *die of freezing* mama!

Compared to this moment—naked in a pile of imagining babies—I have never cared that much about god.

Winter

I imagine the snow falling as sonar.

I imagine the snow falling as drones. I imagine the snow falling as recognition, as having something to do with souls, I. The house smells like poop all day, it's given from all directions. It's—

Winter

I told you a hundred times mama:

Dark Vader on my penis.

Yoda on my penis.

Luke Skywalker on my penis.

Not all these guys on my butthole.

Christmas Genital Self-Examination

This morning: undifferentiated wonder about the children,
undifferentiated wonder about the snowman they just made,
undifferentiated wonder about the insides of ourselves—

and nothing of my soul translates into cynicism.

My tiny son yells through the locked door No is very cold!

Yes love, the snow is very cold!

Just as this mirror in my hand is very cold. The mind of winter—she is
referring to the Diagram of Visible and Invisible Female Genitalia:

and, nothing herself, beholds nothing that is not there and the
nothing that is.

In the mirror: my soul, some ordinary bread, a pretty rug in front of
the fire, this nation-state's drones killing someone right now, a river
flowing down a valley into an estuary, and terror in the plain pink.

It's so cold that I've both turned on the heat in the bathroom and lit a
fire in the living room. The door is locked, the children are pounding
on the door.

I'm going to be alone in this room for ten minutes, I tell my soul.

I say to my soul: don't move toward the pounding door.

I say to my soul: one has to learn to love, and *to be loved.*

Stop pounding on the door I am doing a genital self-examination in
here! what's a genital self-examination mama it's when I look at my
vulva and butthole in the mirror oh!

The vulva is the part you can see right mama? that's right sweetie stop
pounding the door okay mama.

The vagina is invisible right mama? so to speak, love.

When are you going to open this door to make the eggs mama? I am never making eggs for you go ask your father okay mama I.

The vulva consists of the outer and inner labia and the clitoris—the admissible, the venerable, the operable, the appropriate, the tenable, the well-founded, the hevel, I—.

Soul, and a woman—practically begging. I pull apart, as far as I can, I.

As, for example, the hinge of the bivalve shell—

and underneath this vulvar—the butthole.

I am looking into the mirror for proof that I am not only what I believe myself to be—

urination occurs through the urethral opening, mama! he yells through the door. I know sweetie thanks! you're welcome!

While vaginal penetration occurs through the family, businesses, and institutions—

built for the protection of this particular kind of genitals I am looking at right now—white. Pinks, beiges, some dark purple, black—and concealing within itself

and revealing from within itself—I—, thin as a parchment.

Do I love looking closely at something I don't understand, until it changes me.

Open the door now mama no.

It's simple to open the door mama—you just turn the knob and it's open mama no.

Loving these children, or, the endless vigil of our intimacy almost to insanity, I.

It's simple mama just open the door! "Simple" means "not composite."

Simple means *made of nothing else.*

In the hand-mirror my genitals are outside the window, where it is snowing again—.

My god how beautiful I.

A child pounds on the door and yells I'm a scared baby pirate so can you hold my hand and kill something for me?

I wrap a towel around myself, open the door, and kill it.

Winter

My third collection of poems, *Faulkner's Rosary*, is published. I wrote the poems while I was pregnant with Oskar and his twin, and then during the days I miscarried Oskar's twin while we were visiting my parents in Missoula over Thanksgiving, and then up until the moment of Oskar's birth in Phoenix.

While pregnant with Oskar I experienced hallucinations. In most of them—I was filled with blood. Filled, entirely, with blood. I was a bag of blood,

and the *blood was loving*. That's what the book is about.

I feel horrifyingly-revealed that that book—filled with such blood and baby-love—filled with *believing that something new was coming out of my sky*—now exists for the world to see.

I don't do a book tour. I do give one interview, because the interviewer is a friend. I burrow more deeply into the peninsula, into the children, into the mud beneath the rains, into the fungal mat that is alive beneath us—that book published, I long to sink into the muddy peninsula, so revealed. Opened,

why am I writing, again, these deepest privacies—for no one, I.

Drones are killing someone right now—I want to feel—just holding this baby in my arms, right now.

I might be pregnant again.

What is coming out of me again—is it a revelation, or am I *being revealed*.

Is being revealed just a necessary cost of loving.

I fucking hate myself right now.

Winter

Todd looks over my shoulder, reads a few lines, says: you're engaged in a lot of mythic thinking.

Years later I ask, as I arrange these pieces into a book, is this poetic: Todd's vasectomy.

When I have too much information, I resort to pattern recognition. I

Winter

If you're going to sit here and kick my computer then you have to get out of this bed.

I said don't do that, not "do it again and again."

Winter

I love driving through the rain at night to teach at the community college. My classes are usually full of high school students who despise high school and are able to get their English credits in my classes instead, and veterans, and women in their twenties who want to try for their associate degree, maybe one or two students who want to transfer to the University of Washington or Evergreen State College just down the road. And a few older people who use the class as a kind of book club.

As ever, I love my students. I love thinking with them about writing in the pitch dark evenings—rain falling all around us—near-strangers sitting together in a fluorescent-lit room, writing out our lives, full and fragile and weird, and I.

I often say to my students: what are you *not* writing about in your poem?

I tell my students that the family-animal they were made from—they could think of it as an infinite and simultaneous and exponentially-growing venn-diagram, laying heavily upon their—.

Anxiety, noise I.

Right now everyone in this house is crying.

Right now everyone in this house is screaming stop.

My aura of lesser colors, or the pile of papers to grade, or

an intrauterine bullet to the mind I.

Christmas Dissociation

Coherence of my thoughts this morning, which—in the deep exhaustion of nursing this baby in front of the fire—I find I'm flickering back and forth between moments of my life. I'm twelve, I'm twenty-seven, I'm thirty-two, I'm four—

I'm switching, in my weariness, and with this fire as my timeless focal-point—between geographies and rooms and homes and many different kinds of brains I once had.

With every brain I've ever had there was a fire, somewhere, that I stared at. And I.

And frustration—*the mind-shattering frustration*—my coffee and journal and pen on the desk, just out of my reach. I'm composing this in my brains while the baby nurses. I will remember some of it, I will forget most of it.

The baby is weighing on my torso like a thick stone column, piercing through my chest, and then pushing through the chair then through the floor of the cabin and then into the forest floor below us. The baby is pinning me to this spot—frustration—such as I have never found a way to convey because simultaneously I am exactly addicted to their.

Milk smells and urine smells I.

Their tiny round toes, the strings of drool sucking in and out of their mouths with the milk I.

Milk flows down his chin while he nurses.

While he nurses he looks at me so hard, so unblinking, so wide, so clear I.

He looks at me as if he is sucking into himself not only milk but *my entire soulface, I.*

Firelight—timeframes switch—when I was little, her brother.

Sticking out his tongue and wiggling it at her as they drive past the high school girl's house and saying, every morning, *I smell pussy.*

Christmas Dissociation

This baby burrows himself back into my body like when I was little, and I buried myself in the snow.

The baby pinches and holds onto the skin of my arm like when I was little, and her brother grabbed at.

When I was little, and he wiggled his fingers and his tongue at her each day when he drove them to and from school, and her other brother just.

When I was little, and her oldest brother sniffed the air each time they passed a particular house as he drove the three of them to and from school.

He said *I smell pussy* and he sniffed. He sniffed the air and said pussy every day when they passed the house, because a high school girl lived in that house.

When I was little, and her brother turned to look at her in the back seat while he was still driving the car, and he sniffed the air to see what her reaction would be.

Or turned toward her in the back seat to stick out his tongue and wiggle it at her slowly and he was still driving the car, but he wasn't looking at the road he was looking at her.

When I was little and he wasn't looking at the road, instead he was looking at her in the back seat and.

He was looking at her to scare her.

While he wiggled his tongue slowly at her, while he was driving and not looking at the road and she.

When I was little, and her other brother in the passenger seat just laughed and shook his head, and sometimes he reached over to take the wheel, to keep the car from going off the road.

When I was little, and the door to her bedroom had a lock, but all you had to do was jiggle it for a few seconds and the door opened.

When I was little, and her friend was afraid to stay overnight.

When storms were a holy time. And the snow was a holy burying.

But right now, the emergencies inside of the babies are a holy time when—

what have I been buried inside of. This snowy valley, where we live right now, is holy to me.

When I was little, and she longed fervently for holy time, then at last we were in Advent and then—could parts of her life—simply fall away.

And could the falling away, be quiet.

I have longed so deeply for this *time outside of time*. For the sacred night, when I can submit to whatever I am buried inside of, I.

And then one night, in that time outside of time of nursing a baby for months or years.

One night in the blur of not-asleep and not-awake for years, the years of nursing a baby, I find myself trying to remember the feeling of a crush.

What is the feeling of having a crush.

What is the feeling of giddy with excitement. What is the feeling of adoring him, a high school boyfriend I.

What was that feeling of anticipation, of dread, of thrill at the thought of.

What was the feeling of winter, when he's just learned to drive and we're in his mom's old volvo wagon and I'm young enough that I'm still excited for Christmas.

We're driving in the snow and it's just the two of us and we pull over, this night cut in half and still drugged, the baby nursing while sleeping across the staples and I can't shake the belief that my intestines and my uterus and my bladder could fall out through my vagina or that the baby will stop breathing or that someone is trying to visit us but can't find their way to our home—and so instead of thinking about those things, I try to remember what exactly was the feeling of that first kiss.

Soft. Drool, his mouth open over my breast and so tender I.

What exactly did the boy's mouth taste of that was so good—a little toothpaste, the smell of the cold snow falling, the boy wearing cologne. And that boy was a good person, and he.

Thinking of the boy's mouth there is now so much milk coming out of my breasts that it runs back out of the baby's sleeping mouth and all the way down my sternum, down to the staples that run between my hips, where I try very hard to remember—what exactly did it feel like to have his hand go there.

What exactly was the feeling of god yes he might touch that, and I.

What exactly was the feeling of being felt up for the first time—the beginning, barely, of moving toward *this*—his one hand under, and I.

And my one hand under the tiny baby's head while he sleeps and sucks, my other hand covering my vulva, and that hand's forearm resting over the c-section staples and my deflated abdomen—so that I am touching all the things of me that are, right now, the most hurt, and I.

Winter

Half-slept and half-nursed all night long—and it rained all night long.

The whole night was a shifting, morphing, suckling, rumbling waking dream in which *I was having thoughts*, and I wanted to remember the thoughts so I could write them down when I woke.

All night long the whole family-animal moved and shifted without ever stilling, without ever dropping off into our separate sleep—and the rain was falling all night.

The rain is still falling this morning—they finally just fell deeply asleep so I was able to leave the bed and come downstairs to write about this feeling of living in a soup. A family-soup. Or a womb, and this valley is the placenta and we.

Our bed and our living room are a thick broth, and we all swim in it.

It's raining so hard. The amniotic insides of this house—where we are floating—

there is the quick, dense communication of our rage that I can hear with my ears—the slams or screams. But there's also an atmospheric communication—we are all connected by some kind of fabric, like water or thick air—and we communicate through the fabric without words or sounds.

Our sleep is like we are all submerged in a house-sized container of pitch-black water, and if I move then everyone can feel the waters around them move, though there is no light or sound.

Knowledges we have of each other—our interiorities and our physicalities and all the things *of us* that abide outside of our bodies, too—knowledges of these things are transmitted back and forth through the liquids and solids and slimes of this family-soup.

It rained all night long and all night long, like whales, we were connected to each other by the fabric of something like water.

So close to each other that I can feel the disruptions of the air or the water, all around me, when someone else in the family-animal is—like right now—they know, because the amniotic fabric shifted—that I have left the bed.

And I know, right now, that they are awake.

It's like hearing with my tentacles. And none of it is *words*.

Is this atmospheric hearing also the way I know that drones are killing someone right now.

It's raining so hard, it rained all night long and the whole cabin smells like water. The tentacles we.

Winter

This morning his arms are wrapped around my neck because he wants me to be as close to him as possible as I kneel before him:

Mama, poop is coming out of my butt.

Okay love.

Does that make you real happy?

Yes.

Christmas Poem

The rain will freeze by evening, and then the whole forest will sparkle.
And then whole trees will shatter with the wind, beautiful I—is he
still screaming about the fucking egg? no—about the yogurt.

One baby is sick one baby is teething, and every few minutes someone
cries. The cry for itch. The one for poop while pooping the one for
poop already pooped. The one for hunger the one for nursed too
much the one for needs to vomit because nursed too much and the
one for gagging on vomit. The one for vomit flavor or vomit coming
out of nose and then the cry because wiping his nose. The cry of relief
because able to breathe and the cry because, after vomiting, hungry
again.

The one—we don't know why, I—there he is. He's crying.

It's okay to be mad sweetie: MQ-1B Predator and MQ-9 Reaper with
sensors and two Hellfire missiles.

Christmas Miscarriage

That there is, perhaps, an exit to the mind. To dropping, slowly, out of the labyrinth.

But the actual exit is dun dun dun dundun dun, dundun dun: the baby hums the Star Wars Imperial March while he nurses

and sucks into himself my entire soulface.   Slipping, we will lose winter, altogether.

Our home, just a few feet away from the melt-off of one of the world's last glaciers: there will be the moment when it actually stops.

To freeze, I tell my son, my hands in the air, is not the same as to stop.

Winter

Modernist American poet Wallace Stevens wrote a famous poem
about winter called "The Snow Man." Over these past few years of
trying to write a poem about winter, I have smashed my head again
and again against his poem about winter. I have smashed my poems
into his poem.

And I have alternately loved and despised his poem:

> The Snow Man
>
> One must have a mind of winter
> To regard the frost and the boughs
> Of the pine-trees crusted with snow;
>
> And have been cold a long time
> To behold the junipers shagged with ice,
> The spruces rough in the distant glitter
>
> Of the January sun; and not to think
> Of any misery in the sound of the wind,
> In the sound of a few leaves,
>
> Which is the sound of the land
> Full of the same wind
> That is blowing in the same bare place
>
> For the listener, who listens in the snow,
> And, nothing himself, beholds
> Nothing that is not there and the nothing that is.

I believe Stevens made a transcendent mistake in his poem "The
Snow Man." Snowman, listen to me—and you, the disembodied male
listener—listen:

> blood fills me *entirely*.

Blood fills the family-animal *entirely*. We do not transcend. We don't have a mind of winter, we have a multi-brained family-animal of winter, and winter is disappearing from earth as the earth warms.

The microbes at the center of each snowflake are the same exact microbes that are inside of the bodies of the family-animal—we are the same thing as everything around us, we—*boom boom* sounds from lego guns upstairs—he's awake.

Our bodies are filled with wifi. Our bodies are filled with pings.

It is two in the morning and I am here to write a poem about winter with my mind of winter, I—

there you are love. Come here. Your toes are freezing.

The Snow Man

With an academic

snowman, I. It's not that my unconscious that is being silenced,

as expounded by Lacan—it's that children are being blown up. Right now, I.

The Snow Man

I am writing these pieces in an effort to place a stable stake into some kind of solid ground—the family-animal is right now so much air and liquid—we are disintegrating into each other, and into the heat of their fevers that I.

Middle of the night—they're 104.2 and 104.4 and both of them are wheezing. It's snowing too hard to drive them to the emergency room.

I bend my face to his to calm one with my breath, as I cool him with a wet cloth, as I hold him with my whole god-face, I— this baby was once an angel with a torch pushing out of me—.

We're still in a health insurance gap while adjunct teaching.

Is the self-torturing mind a kind of happiness.

Rulers of This World, you can't have my maternity.

Aporia doesn't get my maternity, G8 nations don't get my maternity, the pipeline doesn't get my maternity, the metaphor doesn't get my maternity, the snowman doesn't get my maternity, the maw doesn't get my maternity, the beginning doesn't get my maternity, mass extinction doesn't get my maternity, ocean acidification doesn't get my maternity, the genital self examination doesn't get my maternity, the health insurance denial doesn't get my maternity, happiness doesn't get my maternity, my attacker doesn't get my maternity, dissolution doesn't get my maternity, transcendence doesn't get my maternity, I.

Rulers of This World, I—look. Look into this hole:

Since the children have been born, the emphatic hole of my life has shifted from cunt to asshole.

Since the children have been born I am always bending over—

Am I picking legos up from off the.

Am I assuming the position of.

Am I bending over to show you something.

Am I trying to open the portal to another.

Am I demeaning something, or am I deepening something, or.

Am I trying to show you that I am innocent.

Does innocence simply mean that I am concealing nothing.

Look: there is nothing that I am concealing.

Look: I am offering you everything I possibly.

So that what is hidden is revealed. So that I—

am I asking you to consider one hole over another, wherein.

Am I trying to repel.

Is this hole the entrance where—you are the mama bird and I am the baby bird, tweet.

You are the mama cow and I am the baby cow, moo—am I showing you how disgusting.

Or how beautiful. Or how what we do for love is—and how love, in the history of this nation state—

who can look inside the holes of whom. Who, in this nation state, must bend over.

Wherein the supreme court ruled that officials can strip-search suspects for any arrest, no matter how minor the offense.

This may involve an Intimate Person Search, during which prison or jail officials look inside of mouths, anuses, vaginas.

Women are forced to spread their legs and spread their labia while a guard peers into their vaginal cavity.

Men lift up their penises and scrotums and, if they're uncircumcised, have their foreskins pulled back.

At this point the guard tells the subject to turn around so they can start again at the top. Now the subject has to ruffle the back of their hair, and bend over with legs spread.

The guard might say "squat and cough" with the aim of dislodging an object stored in the rectum or vagina.

The strip-search ends with the subject's being asked to show the bottoms of their feet.

The bottoms of their feet—wherein, what has appeared, holy, there.

Your beautiful little feet, oh!

What beautiful baby toes. My god I.

Winter, late morning, sunshine

Not right now love, I'm writing.

He is crying very hard on the other side of the door while he tries to say mama can you open the door.

I started writing late today and the sunshine is reflecting so brightly off of the snow that it hurts to look toward the window—all the divisible moments I.

I open the door to let him in—take my shoe off mama, itch my foot.

So I take off his shoe and I itch his foot oh my fucking god he is so sweetly soft. And the smell of his stinky little foot I—don't get mad at me mama. No.

No I won't get mad love. I want to eat this stinky little foot I.

Oh my fucking god we are sitting on the floor in the sunshine coming through the window and the glare of the snow is blinding us and I am scratching his itchy stinky little foot and we are smiling so hard

at each other we are smiling so hard in the middle of the smell of his stinky foot and we are so happy. We are so happy.

I am so happy.

I am so happy.

Winter

The bedrooms on the second floor of the cabin are painted lemon yellow and robin's egg blue, each with a large window next to the bed, overlooking the creek. No one ever seems to sleep in the blue room, though it is set up for the children. We all sleep together in one enormous bed in the yellow room.

Since Mateo has been born there are now so many moments in the middle of the night that Oskar holds onto my back while I turn away from him to nurse the new baby.

While I nurse this new baby I reach my top arm back behind myself to hold onto tiny Oskar. Before Mateo arrived, I had never turned my back to him.

How painful and tender, across the years, our nights—

How much happens between us as we sleep, maneuver, shift, dream, breastfeed, leak, tangle, untangle, cry, comfort, check on each other, make dream noises, fever, read books, listen to the salmon spawning in the creek below, listen to the owls, listen to the rain, wait to fall asleep, despair of no sleep, sleep.

And wake.

It truly is a betrayal to the babies, then, after a night of our deeply active caring, and the so many kinds of communication between us— that I wake up without them and leave the bed before they do.

The babies are so pissed at me on the mornings that I untangle myself from their warm little legs and their perfect smells,

so pissed that I sneak off—instead of re-entering the waking world with them, entangled and warm with them.

This morning I left them, to walk down the stairs, to make a cup of coffee, to think about winter, I—he's awake.

He's at the top of the stairs, right now.

Christmas Poem

The tiny new baby is nursing and falling asleep in my arms.

The bigger baby is moaning behind him, spooning the tiny new baby. His arms are reaching around the tiny baby toward me, but he can't reach me, and now he's silently crying.

The pain we feel, about this other baby, between us.

The Snow Man

I beg winter to freeze us. To stop us   *right here.* This

tangle, or this depletion, or this rage— this

perfectly reverberating winter. This one. I

Winter, a few years later

What happens if I smear a single question across time—who is innocent, and for how long. What makes us.

What of ours is our own.

Is it still possible—in this world—to have a soul.

What if I extend my question across years, and across thousands of attempts to write a poem.

What if, instead of a compression or a culling of language—I push and I push at the same questions until, in the *surplus*, in thousands of failed poems about winter, collected across many winters, I—.

I often say to my students—push at that harder. And—think about that harder.

I say to my students—push your thought until you discover what is behind that thought.

I say to my students—smash something together.

I often say to my students: subject your largest questions to the *dimension of time.*

For many years now, I have thought about winter, and I have thought about my children, and I have thought about the invisible wars that our country is always waging, and I have thought about time.

I cannot, from our home in Los Angeles, not right now, hear the salmon thrashing outside of my window—

I cannot know what the salmon just accomplished, across time.

This year I've heard that the orcas are starving and pods are dwindling—no new calves survived in this generation.

I have always associated the human soul with dwindling.

I have always associated the human soul with a fire burning in a small cabin in the middle of the woods—snow piled up all around. An ocean not too far away.

I have always associated the human soul with a woman sitting in that cabin at her computer, trying to write a poem about winter. A baby is nursing on her lap while she types with one hand. Another tiny boy plays with something behind her, and he is talking to her. She's weary, but she is deeply happy, and she has a cup of very strong coffee with just a little cream. It's still too hot to drink, so she can't really think yet. Instead she looks at the internet.

Snow is blowing gently. It's still mostly dark out.

Mama, you do it, you open the door no.

You open the door no. Do it no. Do it no. Do it no.

It's still too dark, love, we'll go outside a little later.

Not only does the intense pounding of naval and industrial sonar mask whale calls over vast stretches of the ocean.

You do it mama you open the door. No. Mama no mama no. For whales I—.

For whales and dolphins there are no noise-cancelling headphones to stop the U.S. Navy's 235-decibel pressure waves of unbearable pinging and metallic shrieking.

At 200 decibels the vibrations can rupture your lungs and above 210 decibels the lethal noise can bore straight through your brain until it hemorrhages that delicate tissue I.

If you're not deaf after the navy's sonar blast then you're dead.

Split and entanglement, and the search for a new human, said Fanny Howe I, you do it mama open the door no.

I have always believed I had a soul, I—hevel.

Christmas Poem, a few years later

Utter destruction can you say that Archie? utter destruction.

Then everybody laughing hysterically. I

The project of the winter poem

The project, then, is to theorize a kind of geo-affect.

The project, then, is to ask: how can I have a soul.

The project, then, is to procure a soul for the babies.

The project, then, is to bend over—

because the project is vulture capitalism.

The project is, inside of myself—to unhook the.

The project is the solution.

The solution, then, is to concentrate—.

The solution is made up of several bodies—bodies that are concentrated inside of and outside of my.

Or, the project is a dilution.

A dispersion, there—is a fire in the fireplace. There is no moon this morning. Mateo just started crawling. Oskar is suddenly reading. We currently have health insurance. I am not, right now, pregnant. No one has a fever.

The Snow Man

The project, then, is to uphold the whale.

The project is not to avoid—but also, to not get trapped.

The project, then, is to show how much bounce and interpenetration—the project is the exhaustion.

The project is to pierce "the prodigious idea."

The project is to show how the night sky is huddling. The mountain is thinking.

There is goodness inside of is he hot? No.

Is that one hot? No.

Question this morning: Am I doing an ok job being your mother? How can I improve?

Oskar's answer: The droids did a terrible job shooting the Jedis and the blaster emissions ricocheted back on themselves.

Exhaustion, I.

Gasping.

Gasping and stuttering with aliveness—I can't think of the right words, I can't remember their names, I.

I'm so worried I might be pregnant.

The Snow Man

My chest hurts I feel such anxiety I can't sleep. The rain is melting the snow.

Our bed is made of bacteria, virus, fungus, mold, bugs, babies, jizz, blood, poop, tears, salt, sodium chloride is the same thing as salt mama. That's true sweetheart now back into your own bed no way mama I'm staying with you I.

I feel such anxiety, I.

Christmas Poem

I'm definitely not pregnant. About three weeks late, and blood all over—he walks in while I'm in the bathroom—he mimics crying.

Same little boy a few minutes later, says: I'm a boy who always worries that you love my brother more than me. But I'm also a boy who wants my brother to be loved. I'm a boy who doesn't need to feel special.

Oh.

Oh my god.

I would walk in front of a mack truck for you I would step off the edge of every world for you I would die all the possible ways for you there are so many people I would kill for you there is much of this world I would destroy for you that I'd explode for you that I'd ruin for you that I'd implode for you that I'd bomb that I'd devastate that I'd cut down that I'd impale that I'd.

What I would do for you, my love, is the drones killing someone right now.

What I would do for you, my love, is the brains of the whales exploding from my military and industrial sonar right now.

What I would do for you, my love, is the prison industrial complex right now, is—I would end health insurance subsidies for the poorest children right now.

What I would do for you, right now, is this fire. Is something baking. Is a pretty rug I.

Focus. Focus. —I:

Winter

It is snowing so hard this morning that I almost wake the children so they can see it.

The snowflakes are large, thick, and slow-motion as they fall—suspended.

It is a silent snow that will quiet the entire forest with its insulation. Lately I have been trying to listen to the forest floor as, I believe, I am always listening to the sonar.

I have been trying to allow the mountain behind our home to enter me, the way I believe the sonar from whales and military and industrial sonar is always entering me, I.

The broader sonic—

the acoustics of this valley. This peninsula. The salmon. This creek. The ocean all around us, I.

My hearing is diminishing, day by day—last week the audiologist re-programmed my hearing aids in order to amplify the sounds and volumes that I can no longer hear.

But I think the hearing aids need to be re-programed again—right now they over-amplify the highest-pitched screeches of the children, so that sometimes I.

I listen to the children all day long—their stories, their questions—I have written down so many thousands of things they have said. Yesterday Oskar almost directly quoted Tao Te Ching 78 when he said "Nothing is softer or stronger than water, everyone in the world knows it—"

and...there he is.

Winter

Where did you get that Mateo?

You should put it on your lips Mateo.

Do you think that is your lips? Well, it's not. That's your chin.

Those are your lips. Do you feel that? Those are lips.

Do you think that is your lips, Mateo? Well, it's not. That is
your mouth.

Your mouth is inside, and your lips are outside, right there.

I'll show you. See? I put it on my lips. It tastes like cherries, but it's
not candy.

Do you think it's candy, Mateo? Well, it's not. You should *not* eat it.

Mama, Mateo is eating the chapstick.

Don't eat the chapstick, sweetie.

See? You should just spread some on your lips, but not eat it.

Now put it on your lips, but don't put the cap in your mouth,

the cap is too small and you might choke. Give me that, I'll just hold
that part.

Do you think that is your lips, Mateo? Well, it's not. That's your hair.

Winter

Mama, Mateo has one of your special medicines.

Looking out from the shower: Mateo, will you put that tampon back, sweetie?

Why?

It doesn't taste yummy.

Oh! Not yummy!

Oskar: No, Mateo, it's not yummy—it's mama's and it doesn't taste yummy.

Mateo rips the shower curtain back, the tampon in his mouth: mama! it's not yummy!

Winter

I can already hear them murmuring upstairs. Todd's trying to keep them in bed so they will fall back asleep, but I just clanked the cup while I was making coffee so—I thought so—there are the footsteps, I.

Christmas is coming the goose is getting fat!, and someone screaming something about breakfast.

I'm going to try to ignore the children and write anyway:

Do I have some questions right here, in the middle of. Screaming.

Someone crying already this morning—something about pooping.

Right in the middle of whatever there is. Frequency, I.

If I could pull or cut something out of myself, and.

A fetal curl is the first shape my body took, so why did I rush past it.

After the first baby was born, the very moment he was placed in my arms, I imagined bending over.

I imagined spreading my butt cheeks as far apart as I could

to reveal—I was practically begging my soul to reveal itself.

The Snow Man

It's been a long stretch of time since I've sat down at this desk.
Respiratory viral infections. More fevers. I've been sick, too.

The children just came back into the house with their hands full of
the perfect metaphor for our contemporary hyper-complexity: poop is
frozen on the eggs mama!

They've been feeding the chickens and gathering eggs with Todd. The
tassels on their brightly colored winter hats are sheathed in ice, their
noses are running, their cheeks are pink, their boots smell like chicken
shit, and they're covered in mud. They're letting in the cold air.

Hey Mateo smell this egg—the chicken poop doesn't stink when
it's frozen!

Hey Mateo smell your boots—the chicken poop *isn't* frozen, so
it stinks.

The boys sniff the eggs and sniff their boots until the poop on the eggs
thaws and begins to stink, too. Oskar's point is proved.

This cabin in the snow—I have attempted to raise it, politicize it,
sabotage it, lament it, embody it, dissolve it.

This cabin is in the snow—

partially or profoundly spread, and I—time. During the days with
these children, time is strange.

The days take so long, I'm so bored, I.

Christmas Dinner

Noises—the underlying moan and the low groan and the soft beg and the grunt of rage and the huff of disapproval and disgust that underlies each of my days, for years.

I'm bouncing this I'm rubbing that I'm.

These are very disapproving people in this house.

These people don't think I'm doing a good job here.

I am operating locally as capitalism, militarism, metallurgy, white supremacy, and environmental degradation I.

Fight your inner woman. Experts say that women tend to be sympathetic—don't be.

History has shown that serial killers and other criminals often play on the sympathies of unsuspecting women in order to lure them into dangerous situations.

Sometimes I long to make a full, complete sentence beautifully crafted because I believe it would indicate something about how my mind.

Sometimes I am so deeply-comforted by fragmentedness. I keep reading and re-reading Roland Barthes' *Mourning Diary,* written after his beloved mother's death. How he—

how *sparse.*

Christmas Dinner

The snow is falling, a fire is in the fireplace, a chicken is baking, the family-animal is inside of the cozy house, it's dinner time, a fire is in the fireplace, the snow is falling, the fire is in the fireplace, something is baking, snow is falling, the family-animal is inside of the cozy house I—

when I eat chicken it's not a chicken so why do you call it a chicken. It *is* a chicken, actually, it's a dead chicken. This is a dead chicken?

So when you give me salmon it's an actual dead salmon yes.

It's a real dead fish—. Yes.

Winter

Christmas came and went so quickly this year. Everyone was sick. The holiness never kicked in.

One could follow the Catholic calendar and feel time to be *almost always sacred*—and it is so delineated: Sacred Time. The other half of the calendar is ordinary—*Ordinary Time.*

I was told, when I was a child, that Ordinary Time was when I was to be subject to dailiness. To mundanity. To my childhood's endurance of the world. And I was supposed to grow my faith from that.

I was told that Sacred Time, on the other hand, was when I should step away from dailiness and remember that earth was but a momentary stop for my soul, I.

But it is this desk I have loved—not time.

It is this snowfall I have loved—not history.

It was my childhood I loved—and not eternity. And not memory.

Christmas Poem

Money, if drones are bombing eight countries right now.

Money, if drones are bombing seven countries right now.

Guns, if we are saturating the world with guns, and if the war is always invisible to me.

If the world is warming because of fossil fuel consumption, so that winter will disappear, then I don't love my own babies.

If Rikers is putting children into solitary confinement for years, then I am not capable of love.

If crude oil begins to flow in pipes beneath sacred waters, then I am not capable of love.

The empire bends her head over her cup of coffee. One baby is 101.2. The boy is 103.2.

Snow falls softly outside. The fire is burning. Something is baking. There is a pretty rug in front of the fire I—

my father wasn't alive on earth this Christmas. Incomprehensible to me that he is no longer on earth.

In order to think clearly, I need something that I don't have.

Winter

Winter night, I haven't slept well in a few days. We're in the middle of an intense cold spell. The wood floor is cold, even through my wool socks.

We've hung thick blankets over the front and back doors to keep out drafts.

The children are warm and growing in the dark room above me while I pace the kitchen and living room.

Firelight causes the windows to reflect me walking back and forth across the room.

I open the front door to watch the snow, to feel the intensity of the cold. It's so cold I can't smell the rotting salmon, the spruce, the fir, the cedar, or the forest soil—they've frozen.

The pressure behind the sternum. The anxiety, I.

Aghast that I could be sleeping, but I am not, I bend over. I give a.

The snowy wind in my eyes—but glory, but self-mercy, but drones, — the state is not wasteful, it uses the entire human.

Winter

The pressure behind the sternum. My anxiety—I often say it like that: *it is mine.*

During the time in which I've been writing these winter rituals early in the morning, milk leaking from my breasts and dazed with exhaustion, I have also been writing essays, finishing a book about traveling for a few months in South America, and I've left the peninsula a handful times to give readings, participate on panels, or present at conferences.

Whenever I leave the peninsula—whenever I leave the babies even for a few hours to go teach—I feel as if I'm being pulled by the arms out of a deep mud, but the bottom half of my body never breaks free— the hips and leg parts of me are left behind, and my insides slowly elongate. I'm eviscerated—as the top half of me travels or teaches. Parts of my insides get caught at the family-animal and,

tugged-out, or trailing guts around behind me.

I recently traveled to Harvard to participate in a panel on sentimentality and poetry. I think I was invited because my last book was about being pregnant with Oskar and his twin, who we lost in the middle of the pregnancy. I was invited to speak about sentimentality because part of this world automatically associates sentimentality with women and babies—though nothing I have experienced with the birth of these babies has been, to me, sentimental. Everything I have experienced has been excruciatingly, and exhilaratingly—glut. Gutted. Exploded. Enormous. Simultaneous. Miniscule.

Incommensurate with my previous brains. Incommensurate with my previous body. Incommensurate with my previous soul. Incommensurate with the parts of this world that automatically associates babies with—anything at all—

104.1. No health insurance right now. I

Winter

104.2 sometimes the anxiety is so intense I—to pull apart something.

I pull at—what is the center that holds—and where the pressure, what release I.

Or, to smash things together so hard that I—what we experience shapes what we are capable of understanding.

So hot, this little one—what if.

What if, seeking consolation.

Is seeking consolation exactly the wrong way to live—

am I seeking consolation.

Winter

The revulsion, I—when I imagine my attacker, he is seven years older than I am, no matter what my age is at the time—when I was ten, he was seventeen.

When I was sixteen, he was twenty-three.

When I was thirty-one, he was thirty-eight.

When I was nine, he was sixteen.

When I was twenty-six, he was thirty-two.

When I was fourteen, he was twenty-one.

When I was eight, he was fifteen.

Sticking out his tongue and sniffing the air: *pussy.*

The children are asleep—am I full of undiscerning wonder.

Am I poor in spirit, and am I seeking consolation.

The Snow Man

The fever has broken. It seems the children fever extraordinarily quickly and often. Sitting next to me, Oskar is drawing a pirate scene somewhere in the Caribbean, and Mateo is drawing snow. We are working—we often work together now, for a few minutes, in the mornings.

Oskar: Mateo, are you the kind of person who writes on other people's pictures?

Mateo: Yeah.

Oskar: Well, do you think it's funny?

Mateo: Yeah.

Oskar: Well, it's not funny.

The Snow Man

Me to the children: In wintertime, the water can be differentiated into snowflakes. The snowflakes can be rolled together and shaped into spheres. The spheres can be stacked on top of each other, so that we can stare at no man—

and reflect upon ourselves.

We are laughing because I said *no man*, like the children say, instead of *snow man*.

And they get the existential joke. We are so happy. Laughter.

Laughter, leaking out of a heart.

The Snow Man

Pressure at the sternum. In a time of.

The genius of late capitalism is that we don't know who to point the finger at, the tentacles of cruelty are so.

Long, omnipresent,

wrapped also around the gray whale—dead after stranding itself on a West Seattle beach, found to have over 20 plastic bags small towels surgical gloves plastic pieces duct tape and more in its system.

A whale's system is made of holy mountains and blood,

a whale's system is all the faces of all the gods, a whale's system is all the words for holiness, a whale's system is little girls on horses swimming through the veins of whales,

and the whale swims up our creek,

and through the pipes below our house,

and the pipes bleed into our glasses of water,

and I drink the water and I say: *My god what can I—. My god what can I—.*

My children are laughing so hard.

The Snow Man

When the baby says it how gentle
the word *wrath*: like wrap. Like path
meandering toward
the center bone. The ribbon
of his little basket, jabbering: *detail.*

No man.

More detail.

Give it coal eyes.

The Snow Man

And after, the long rain. And after that, a simple break in the snow falling—remember: thrumming, mingling, wind-swept, once when there was *only my mind,*

and no other mind. This excruciatingly exquisite baby is in my arms, right now. With his unwavering headlong intensity he stares into my soulface. He pulls and pulls *my entire soulface* into himself with his mouth, I—James Mitchell and Bruce Jessen,

it says here that you were paid 180 million dollars by our nation state for your system of torture. He pulls me into himself so hard that I actually gasp, I—.

Christmas Poem

Predators are good liars.

Predators are good at staging a false reality.

If an assailant wants you to go with him somewhere—you have to do everything in your power to prevent a predator from taking you to a secondary crime scene. Once he gets you alone, there may be no way to escape.

So if that means screaming, do it. A high-pitched, animal scream.

Hey guys don't *yell* if a bad guy is getting you—*scream*. Practice both and see the difference.

Who wants to hurt me mama?

Did you say who wants to hurt you?

Christmas Poem, a few years later

Since my dad died sometimes I miss him so intensely that I *become him.* I look out from my own eyes and I am looking at the world *as him.* And I see these children as my grandchildren and—for a moment it feels like I have not utterly lost him

—the mind tries, and it hurts—.

Tonight the points that were snowflakes stopped still—

then blurred into long lines and so now we are moving,

like in the original Star Wars, at light speed will you stop

yelling "mama!" I'm not yelling "mama" I'm role-playing that I'm *screaming* "mama."

You said that I should *scream*, not yell.

I did say that, love.

I said if you are lost, sit down, wherever you are, and scream out my name—my first and last name.

Winter

If we all simultaneously stopped believing in the concept of
nation state.

If we are alive together in this cabin in the forest, drinking glasses of
water with blood in it and looking at each other as if to say—what
should we do?

If I tell my children: you are alive in a beautiful world.

If I tell my children: you are alive in a nation state that tortures, steals
children away from their parents at the border, and wages invisible
war—there are rulers of this earth who—

there are bad people in this world, I tell my children—but you are
alive in a family that loves you.

And, I tell my children: you are alive during a geological time called
The Sixth Wave of Mass Extinction—this forest all around you
is dying.

This ocean all around you is dying—but I am holding you in my arms,
right now.

You are safe, I tell my children, in this home that is made from the
bodies of dead trees.

I tell my children: you have souls.

I say to my children: if we had souls.

I am living with a brain in which the knot on the tiny baby's head from
his brother's fire truck fills me with more terror than all of
winter dying.

More terror than all the invisible wars.

I am living with a brain in which a glass falling to the floor and
shattering elicits a physical reaction in me much greater than my
physical reaction to the baby whale who, confused by or fleeing naval

and industrial sonar, swam from the ocean into the strait then through the inlet and then partway up this creek to die.

I am living with a brain in which a baby poking his finger again and again at my computer screen causes me to scream aloud,

but reading on that computer screen about the child Kalief Browder who is put into solitary confinement in Rikers for three years without a trial and unable to make bail after allegedly stealing a backpack does not make me scream aloud—

but my soul.

My soul when I.

The Snow Man

We are no longer in *human time,* we're in animal time.

We don't have anywhere to go today. No classes. No teaching. No errands. No visits. We'll be here all day long.

It is raining—it's been raining for days. I don't want my portions of life to be deciphered—we often walk out to the creek, the children adorable in their hats and boots, to watch the baby whale decompose across this winter. Its eyes and intestines pulled out by birds,

then its bones gathered by humans. This unrelenting,

this psychic pinging, I. Laughter.

Laughter.

Why are the children laughing so hard.

The Snow Man

It is five in the morning, and I am here to write a poem about winter with my mind of winter.

It begins: *Think of misery in the sound of the wind*—Good morning mama. Good morning love!

Hey mama I see you are writing about a snowman. I am.

I see you are writing about a butthole, too. Yes I am love.

Mama, write: inside of your butthole are chunks of coal, shriveled apples, stones, bolts, electrical fuses, bottle caps, pebbles, champagne corks, and flashlight batteries for its eyes. Okay.

Also write inside your butthole are twigs. Okay.

Also write inside your butthole are carrots, corncobs, buttons, and clothespins for its nose. Okay.

Also write a derby hat and corncob pipe. Do those go in the butthole too? Yes mama.

Okay.

Thank you mama.

Thank *you*. My love.

The Snow Man

It's 2 in the morning. One baby is tangled along my legs and one is still attached to my nipple. I am trying to write in bed so I don't wake them—they've been in and out of fevers. They just fell asleep.

I can see both stars and the snowfall outside this bedroom window. I know the fire is burning in the room below. And I know there is a pretty rug in front of the fire—just as I know the drones are probably killing someone right now.

The term *drone* was coined because of the resemblance of the "loud-and-regular" motor sounds of the early unmanned military aircraft to the male bee—I unlatch the baby.

I stand up, bend over, and spread my butt cheeks as far apart as I can to show you something.

To pull apart something, I.

I pull at what is the center that holds—and where the pressure, what release I.

What if, seeking consolation.

What if seeking consolation is exactly the wrong way to live.

Am I seeking consolation.

Today my attacker turns forty-four.

The most common mistake a woman can make that will result in her getting kidnapped, attacked, and/or raped: getting into the attacker's car when he pulls a gun and orders you to get into his vehicle.

Most attackers don't want to shoot you, they want you to get into the car so that they can drive you to a deserted place and torture you.

Don't comply. Run screaming.

More likely than not, he will just move on to an easier target.

Wallace Stevens wrote that the nobility of poetry is a violence from within that protects us from the violence without. He says that *the imagination* pushes back against the pressure of reality.

Stevens is always so close to being right.

But his "within" and "without" are two closed systems—imagination (inside oneself) and reality (outside oneself)—appear, in his formulation, to have impermeable and durable membranes between them.

I visualize two balloons when I read Stevens' formulation—one balloon is my imagination, and the other balloon is my reality. They slowly push into one another, morphing but not breaking. Sometimes my imagination balloon seems stronger, and it pushes deeply into the roundness of my reality balloon. Sometimes my reality balloon engulfs my imagination balloon. All this time, both balloons stay intact.

But Stevens is singular, insular, too individual, too unbroken, too impermeable, too wry—he's a smug transcendent. He's too much a winner. He's too inviolate. He's—

Stevens' formulation of Imagination vs. Reality feels like mildly pushing two barbie dolls together —softly rubbing two closed-system matrices without permeating, or destroying, or dissolving, or solving anything—

I just want to smash everything together and break everything, I.

Stevens' formulations of Reality and Imagination remain too whole to feel like this world,

even when he writes lines so seemingly-dissolutive as "one must have a mind of winter" or "the listener, who listens in the snow, And, nothing himself, beholds Nothing that is not there and the nothing that is" in his poem "The Snow Man."

I used to love the paradox of these lines—I loved the speaker's apparent willingness to lose his human individuality into the meshes of Geological Time, or Winter, or Nothingness.

But dissolution isn't what happens for me in that poem anymore—

all I can feel in Stevens' poem, right now, is someone not hearing any misery.

The Snow Man

Snow exists somewhere between theory, art, and action.

One of them says to his brother: Are you scared of this snowman?
Yeah. Then I'll kill it for you.

Winter

I am writing about writing a book that is no longer here. I've written over it, I.

Noises, I—.

Stop.

Winter

No one comes to visit us is that another diarrhea. We better start writing these down.

2:30 am boy diarrhea; 2:30 am boy at 103.2; 2:30 am baby at 102.8; 2:35 am for boy ibuprofen; 2:55 am boy at 103.4; 2:55 am baby at 103.4; 2:55 am baby acetaminophen; 3:15 am boy at 102.6; 3:15 am baby at 102.0; 3:25 baby diarrhea; 3:40 am baby 102.0; 3:40; diarrhea

for the boy; 4:00 am 101.4 and diarrhea baby; 6 am 102.1. This goes on for days—.

Christmas Poem

Todd comes downstairs and starts making himself some tea, and pancakes for the boys. It's a Saturday. His dad will come over today to help him with the firewood. His mom is bringing a smoked salmon, Oskar and Mateo's favorite.

Despite all my safety, my luck, and all this love around me—when the first baby was born I began to pray as well as to beg, as well as to want to kill even more enemies: education policy makers shrimp boat captains World Bank executives Monsanto military sonar experts executives at health insurance companies anyone who makes the precariousness not stop.

I began the long supplication, but also—I am even more ready to kill.

Dismember or mutilate I.

I began months of never quite asleep, never quite awake, and ready to kill the drone operators drone designers drone engineers drone profiteers drone apologists and anyone having anything to do with human sonar deployment in the oceans.

Beautiful snow and morning time.

People are coming over today who love us.

The movement from my reptilian brains back to my—.

Oskar walks by, looks over my shoulder and says hey you know mama a lot of neuroscientists no longer believe in the reptilian brain theory I.

Christmas Poem

Mateo are you saying *ankle* or *a-hole*.

Angel.

Laughter.

Laughter.

We're all laughing so hard.

Winter

Oskar is four and a half, and Mateo will turn two after Christmas. I just left them with Todd upstairs, all of them asleep in a pile on our bed, with a thick, slow snow falling in the window behind them.

Beautifying the nightlong cuddle we.

The semester is over. We don't currently have health insurance. And I'm not sure if or what I'll be teaching after winter break.

Todd is driving all over the peninsula to various community colleges to teach, but neither of us have been given a schedule that qualifies for health insurance. I teach at the closest community college, just down the road, two evenings a week, and twice weekly I drive an hour and a half to Tacoma to teach early-morning classes there.

While writing these winter pieces during the past three years I've also finished two other books—those books were *possible to finish*.

This book is being made alongside the children, making themselves while I.

And therefore I cannot imagine how to stop *these* writings. To stop these writings would be akin to admitting that someday their childhood will stop, as my childhood has possibly stopped.

When we checked yesterday, the creek was completely frozen so Oskar wants to try to slide around on it today. I am downstairs by the fire, and my coffee is right in front of me.

The Christmas tree is in the corner between two windows, the windows are full of snow, and they are also reflecting the lights of the tree.

Christmas Party

I'm not really ever asleep and not really ever awake for a few years,
and the Christmas tree sparkles in the dark.

I wonder how to convey *how tired,* sometimes, I.

I wonder—if I possessed sensory organs that could perceive the
interaction of the pinging from the naval and industrial sonar around
our peninsula—would that visualization of a brain-crushing sound
actually be beautiful.

Trusting people to be alone with your children.

This is a difficult one, because child molesters end up being the last
person the parents would believe is the molester.

Most child molesting cases involve a stepfather, the uncle, the sister's
boyfriend, the mother's boyfriend, the grandfather, the babysitter,
the neighbor, the family friend, the youth camp director, the day care
worker, the church volunteer, etc.

When it comes to your children, be suspicious of everyone, no matter
who they are.

We wish we had a soul, instead we have the Corrections Corporation
of America. And mouths. And anuses.

I wish I had a soul, instead I have an attacker.

The crucial thing, I tell the children as we arrive at the Christmas
party, is our contempt.

Christmas Poem

We wish we had souls but instead we have a military industrial complex, a prison industrial complex, a university industrial complex, I.

It is silently snowing in the dark, all is calm. He's at 103.3, but it's dropping.

Christmas Party

Let yourself be kidnapped by a contemporary hyper-complexity—

no one who loves their own child would refuse that nine-year-old her abortion.

The crucial thing, I tell the children, is that our bodies go limp and heavy when they drag us away.

The crucial thing is—don't answer the door, don't walk to the car alone, know your full name, know your mother's phone number.

I say to my children: there are bad people. And, at the family reunion: do not lose sight of me.

I say to my children that adults shouldn't ask children for help. Or: run for your lives.

If, I say—then scream fight gouge the eyeballs punch them in the throat then rip off the balls with your teeth I.

Don't yell, love—*scream*. Practice both right now so you know how they are different.

The little boys sing together at me for a long time Skeleton brain I.

Monsanto—there is an *actual holy mountain*, behind our home.

Snow is falling on it, right now.

Christmas Poem

I want to show myself acting innocently while avoiding the pious arc
of redemption.

I want to show that there is no redemption—I'm practically begging
my money to reveal itself.

I want to show that I am hiding nothing:

Mateo is 104.1, 2:45 a.m. a dose of ibuprofen cool washcloth on his
forehead, some lavender oil on the bottoms of his feet.

I don't want this—*thick of our life*—deciphered.

The Snow Man

The mind breaks as I hold a cool cloth to this child's forehead, another cool cloth on his feet. 104.0

The projectile of this book, then, is to re-imagine the human mind after the magnetic poles have flipped.

When winter is gone from earth, the project is: re-scale, re-calibrate, re-orient, and re-mind.

Mateo says: mama here is the map to your heart—he gestures to his own heart—

mama, it's *eating across my body.*

Christmas Poem

The fever has broken—I am Luke Skywalker and you are Princess Leia. Okay.

Will you wipe my butt Princess Leia? Yes I will Luke Skywalker.

Thank you for wiping my butt Princess Leia. You are welcome Luke Skywalker.

You have a beautiful face when you watch me poop mama. Thank you.

You have a beautiful face, too. And you have a beautiful heart, you're such a beautiful brother, you're such a beautiful friend, you're my beautiful son, you're so kind and you have such beautiful eyes, you have a beautiful gap where you lost your front tooth, and you're full of such beautiful laughter! your laughter is filled with a beautiful light and you also have a beautiful fury and such a beautiful rage that is filled with your beautiful love. I like you so much.

Will you write that on there? Yes.

You could add that I have nice breath. Yes, what else? tell me all the things that you have that are nice and I'll write them down. I've got cute toes. Yes. And fingers. Yes. Write yes. Yes. Laughter. Yes. Anything else? I've got a beautiful voice. You do.

I'm thinking. You said okay write okay. Okay. Because we're writing everything that we say. I'm gentle. Yes. I love animals. Yes. Animals love you, too. Of course they do I've got a very gentle heart. You *do* have a gentle heart, Mateo. I've got beautiful arms. You do. You said mmm-hmmm write mmm-hmmm. Mmm-hmm. Laughter

Laughter.

Laughter.

Christmas Dinner

Mama did you ever notice the irony of "pacific theater."

Pacific means *peace* but it was actually a war, get it? yes I do.

Theater means to *pretend at war* but they were actually *doing* the war, get it? Yes love.

I do.

Mama whenever someone says office I want to hear orifice, do you get it?

I do.

Christmas Dinner

I am facing the world no I'm pooping.

Somewhere, there are people in offices.

Christmas Poem

There was a time in their lives when each of my children have run naked from the bath and they found me, wherever I was, and they bent over. They spread their butt cheeks as far apart as they could to show me something.

Laughing. Laughing so hard it was a gesture of—hilarity. Trust. Joy.

Why do we want *someone to see inside of us.*

Why do we want to *look inside of each other.*

What does it mean to be, or to remain, *intact*—.

When my sons were inside of me—they were *entirely inside of me.*

When my sons were inside of me—they did open their eyes.

Winter

It's pouring rain, and so cold in the cabin this morning. The fire is smoky and won't burn well because I used the new wood that Todd's dad just cut yesterday and piled outside the back door. The dry firewood that would burn better is in the shed outside.

A few weeks ago Todd and I decided to apply to PhD programs because we need to find a better way to have health insurance—right now Mateo is 103.4 and Oskar is 103.2 and they both have respiratory viral infections. We have a catastrophic insurance plan that doesn't cover illnesses. I am not pregnant.

It is raining so hard the day of the exam that the valley is predicted to flood, so we leave a few hours early for Tacoma to take the GREs. Mike and Lindy watch the boys.

While taking the written portion of the GRE I see through the false premise of the prompt, I re-arrange the assumptions underlying the prompt, and then write the essay from that point on. I've nailed it. I've blown the test out of the water. I feel awesome about my performance on the written test.

A few weeks later my scores reveal that my writing portion has scored in the 18th percentile—I've dramatically failed the written portion of the GRE—a test result I will send in with my applications to PhD programs for Literature and Creative Writing.

Update: Todd and I both received acceptances to the University of Southern California's PhD program. I'm torn about whether or not we should move to Los Angeles—our Dungeons and Dragons group has been meeting weekly in this cabin for a few months now, and the campaign is really heating up.

I'm lonely here. The colleges we teach at are broken here. It's so beautiful here. We can't seem to make all the pieces work here 103.5 and 103.3, I—

we find reasons to leave.

Two weeks after we move to Los Angeles, and one day before classes start for our PhD program, I miscarry thirteen weeks into a still-secret pregnancy. My USC health insurance policy kicks in the next day, and our old policy—without our knowing it—had dropped all maternity benefits. Still unsure if I'm miscarrying or not, and in tremendous pain, I go to the emergency room of the hospital where, almost two years later, Archie will be born.

In the ER they give me some fentanyl and thick pads to sit on when, a few minutes after I arrive, I begin to bleed. I'm still bleeding a week later when the fetus falls out into the toilet, and I scoop it out.

I bleed for another two months after that. Thick cords of blood and mucous and tissue, as if I'm finally turning inside-out the way I've often imagined I would.

I stop bleeding around the time we receive the $13,000 bill for the one-hour ER visit, the fentanyl, and the pads.

A few weeks later, for a Christmas gift, Todd gives me several books by Clarice Lispector, who wrote "Now I am going to stop for a while to deepen myself more. Then I'll be back."

In the margin I wrote *lol*.

I had scooped up the fetus from the blood-filled toilet, and I'd held it in my hands—

I spend the next seven years of the PhD researching fetus images in literature, architecture and art.

Winter

The PhD doesn't enter my soul the way books sometimes enter my soul. But the PhD gives us time. It gives us health insurance. It gives us more stability than we'd yet felt as adults. And we do write and read for those seven years—their father just put the plume on the children's new lego knight, and his lego competence makes me want to fuck him.

Before we go to the beach, safety tips for children: children should know their own name—their first and last name.

Say it: what is your first and last name.

Children should know their address. Know their parents' phone number.

If your child is too young to know your name and phone number, write them in your child's shoes. Then, role-play a scenario in which the child should show a stranger their shoe.

Why am I making this attempt to sustain contact with the outside world,

why am I attempting to inject some light and air into *these densities*— these notes from the thick of our family-animal's thickest life, I.

Before we walk to the beach let's role-play. You're lost. Don't yell— *scream*. Sit down on the ground, right now, and scream out my name.

My first and last name.

Winter

I am embarrassed by how much I want another baby.

I feel certain there is another baby. There are possibly a couple
early miscarriages—by which I mean that my period is late, then it
arrives heavy. My period becomes scattershot. For a few months I no
longer know how to time having sex to either become pregnant or to
purposefully not become pregnant. We don't really know what we—.

Oskar and Mateo are joyful, hilarious, tiny, enormous, passionate, and
always-costumed as pirates or knights or bad guys at the beach. At the
park. At the Museum of Natural History across the street from USC.
At the La Brea Tar Pits. At the Malibu Creek State Park. At beaches
and hikes all over Los Angeles. In Los Angeles, I am full of joy and
anxiety. I love these months and years, these thicknesses. *All this light,*
especially after the dark wetness of the peninsula.

We do have health insurance, right now. I am pregnant, right now.

Oskar and Mateo are, right now, running in and out of the waves
shooting at each other with their fingers.

Male children: all wet with my public offerings.

I give unto the non-round technology of the modern world: my sons.

I give unto the non-round technology of the modern world: some
socialized white humans, some pre-drones.

I give unto the non-round technology of the modern world: citizens of
the dark waters. Citizens of the fetal marble.

Citizens, with supremely confident aim I.

Christmas Miscarriage

I am in the middle of coursework and I absolutely love Lee Edelman's book *No Future*, and I, too, am enraged by the ways in which white children and their future are used as symbolic weapons aimed at anyone who is not a wealthy heteronormative pseudo-religious monster while the majority

of actual children on earth are in fact devoured

at the cogs of neoliberal late-capitalism—devoured exactly by those wealthy heteronormative pseudo-religious

monsters who are hypocritically crying out "for the children" — in the middle of a miscarriage,

this morning, the ocean is too bright.

Too reflective. And somewhere inside me a head is still floating.

But it will emerge, like Real Life.

A muscle or something torn so centrally, so utterly internally, that I can't quite place where it hurts, but I.

Winter, a few years

In late May Archie is born.

I've just finished my coursework for the PhD. I have a semester of parental leave from USC. I will prepare to take my comprehensive and qualifying exams in December. This is the year that my father dies. This is also the year I begin to experience vertigo, and to lose much more of my hearing. This is the year I decide there will be no more humans living and dying inside of me.

But in this exact moment—my parents have arrived at our apartment to meet Archie.

The apartment is so small they have nowhere to sit, so they sit on the floor and hold him in their arms and fall in love with him as we have fallen in love with him. My dad is not feeling well, so my mom and Todd take turns walking to the park and beach with Oskar and Mateo. My parents begin to look for a larger place for us to live.

When Archie is four months old we move into a small house a few minutes away from the apartment, in Venice. There is a tiny front yard and a back yard. The ocean is seven blocks away—and Archie is finally here on earth.

We are all here, so Todd has a vasectomy. We are so happy.

I am embarrassed, by how much life, I.

There are many hundreds of winter fragments written during this timeframe that I've chosen to leave out of the book—what we call the *vertigo years*.

For three years after Archie is born—starting just before my dad dies, then across the year that Todd and I take our doctoral exams, then across the years we write four dissertations between us, across the years we teach several classes each, and across the year we live in West Africa for Todd's Fulbright grant for poetics and translation, and my USC research grant—I experience increasingly- frequent episodes of vertigo.

I have had progressive and significant hearing loss my whole life, but across these years I lose much more of my hearing.

During the vertigo episodes the spinning is simultaneously vertical and horizontal, as if my brains are a centrifuge, and the episodes last for up to eighteen hours. Usually they last about six hours. During the vertigo episodes I shit myself, I vomit, I have to lie on the floor in the dark with my eyes half-open, I crawl across the floor instead of walk. Sometimes Todd places Archie on my chest to nurse while I'm spinning. For a few days before and after the vertigo episodes I experience aural and visual distortions, extreme nausea, tinnitus, brain fog, sensitivity to light and noises—but at the same time, an extremely diminished hearing.

Todd's mom consults an intuitive healer on my behalf, and the healer imagines a too-solid, too-large, perfectly clear crystal that abides where my brains should have been, and I.

Eventually a woman who practices traditional Chinese medicine, using a combination of herbs, acupuncture, and food— slows the vertigo enough for the membranes around the spiral-shaped cochlea in the bony labyrinth of my ear—they think—to heal, and I.

What I have left out of this book is

the exquisiteness of this time, in which I.

Christmas Poem

We fly from LA to Montana to spend Christmas with my parents. My
father will die in a few weeks. This is the last time I will ever see him
in this home that he has loved—this home where he was my father.
This home surrounded by mountains, evergreens, a few raggedy
horses in the fields. The snow all around him. The trees outside
weighed down with the thick snow. A fire in the fireplace.

My father, right now, is holding my baby. He is trying to stay alive for
the surgery he hopes to have for his heart this January in Denver. He
will die in the hospital in Denver, and his family will be all around
him.

My father is exceedingly gentle. He has taught me, with all the actions
of his life, about holding oneself in right relation

to the gallery of living and breathing, and also the dead commotion:
there is, perhaps, nothing

more holy to me than this snow falling right now.

Snow and my children. Or, shamelessly, these snow-covered trees
holding themselves

aloof from the snow-covered ground until—bending,

bending, bending—

and we're broken at it, I.

Winter

My father had his first heart open-heart surgery when he was twenty-six, a few months after my older sister died. My mom was pregnant with me—

I have always felt that I was fully-created within the warm pool of their grieving. I have always felt that some ratio of tenderness and sadness is the most loving state of being, to me.

My parents' brokenheartedness has always manifested itself in an overwhelming pressure bearing down on my sternum—a pressure that, since I was a child, I have imagined as a large man standing on me, balanced on one leg, his foot lengthwise down my sternum.

A pressure that I have felt across my entire life, even as a baby.

I remember being a baby, waking up in a crib, and trying to turn my head but unable to because of the pressure on my sternum and neck—I cry, my father enters the room, light from the hallway behind him when the door opens, he picks me up, the pressure releases and my head turns—the memory is over.

The long thick scars down his sternum where across the years they cracked the length of the bone four times, pulled apart his ribcage, and stopped his heart, to fix it.

But your heart, we always joked with him, is perfect.

I have my dad's large Czech nose and prominent cheek bones. And his love of winter.

And sometimes, when I look out from my own eyes, when I am actually him.

Winter

Socio-uterine configurations of—*mama*—something interrupts me,
more completely than I.

Archie toddles into the living room where I am sitting down to write a
poem about winter.

He is super fucking excellent—

he's wearing bright fuchsia sweatpants, an argyle sweater-vest in
greens and golds, and has black permanent marker all over his face
"for decoration."

An interruption-needle so long and quick to the center-brains: the
word *mama*.

That breaks all my concentration completely *mama*, I.

Does any of this matter, I

Winter

Oskar says mama—write: in all, the Mongols only had three defeats during their attacks and conquests.

Write: Their only great defeat was at Japan but they almost won even there. Write that. Okay love—I wrote that.

Write: The Mongols were very victorious. Did you write that? I did, love.

Mama I always think of my immune system like Constantinople. And I think of the germs that manage to take over my body and that I will eventually die from as the Turks, because they managed to overtake Constantinople. That's probably when I will have rabies or the plague or HIV.... My skin is the walls of Constantinople. The white blood cells of my immune system are a strong Byzantine army. My entire body is the Byzantine Empire. My cells are the great in-sides of that walled city. My blood is the Byzantine weaponry.

Did you write all that mama? I did love.

Will you take my temperature?

Winter

If I am liquefying, then so is my writing.

If I am disintegrating, then so is my writing. If I am a family-animal made up of many brains and many legs and many hungers and many poops and many sleeps and many arms, then so is my writing. If I am living in a world in which Donald Trump is the president who grabs pussies, then so is my writing.

If I am living in a nation state that is bombing someone right now, then so is my writing, I.

Todd translates Francophone West African poetry in which, interestingly, *white bread* and *snow* often function as references to colonization, colonizers, Europeans, and North Americans—the white of the snow and coldness of the ice and snow invoking the frozen hearts and the dead-cold minds of old and new colonizers, and the actions they.

Archie, who has never seen snow, asks mama is the snow like tiny tampons?

Did you say is the snow like tiny tampons? yes.

Yes it is.

Winter

I often tell my students who are hesitant to write about their own family: you have a loyalty problem.

I often tell my children: our family-soil contains our petrol sponge, our disposable populations, and the longevity of our radiation.

I tell my children: a mutilated oil is in my books, is in my bowels, is in my pipes, is in my garbage that I—back to bed *right now* my beautiful lovey I will be there in a minute to read with you—a mutilated oil is my fertile spaces.

A mutilated oil is my sacred-accursed.

A mutilated oil is my agro-metaphysical. A mutilated oil is my glut. A mutilated oil is my utero-compulsive, I— Oskar walks by and says hey mama you know Homer called Proteus the "old man of the sea" and I say yes.

Yes, I know. From the bathroom Archie screams: wipe my butt.

He screams out my full name—my first and last name.

Winter

What I'm leaving out of the book: the dozens and dozens of early morning pieces that reflect the children's obsessions—star wars, minecraft, adventure time, magic: the gathering, pirates, knights, wild cats, raptors, the byzantine empire, nordic mythology, arctic baby animals, geology, space-time, astral physics, mad libs, shakespeare, x-files, world war one, world war two, the revolutionary war, all the wars.

Mama he obviously has poop so get off your crap computer and help him.

Christmas Poem

Did Archie say the summer wind would shoot us down? No mama, he said the submarine would shoot us down.

What are you drawing, Dark Vader? No.

Are you drawing Constantinople? No.

Are you drawing a tumbling of continuous variations with fuzzy borders, and with many imperfections in the array? *No!*

Oh, yes: snow.

The genius of late capitalism is the impossibility of identifying at whom, exactly, I'm enraged—

and if I could focus my rage, I—

if I don't look at my baby and think of Kalief Browder, then I don't actually love my baby.

When I have too much information, I resort to pattern recognition: stalemate in my brains I.

Winter

We move to Abidjan, Cote d'Ivoire after we finish up our coursework and all the exams at USC. Todd has a Fulbright fellowship to allow him to work on the translations of several books of Ivorian poetry. I have a research grant from USC so that I can finish my two dissertations.

Todd's mom sends a string of Christmas lights, legos, and vitamins to us through the mail, and the customs fees cost us over three hundred dollars. We drape the lights over a chair in the living room of our apartment and spend Christmas day at the beach with Todd's dad, who has come to visit for a couple weeks.

While living in Abidjan, Archie is two years old, and he begins speaking French with an Ivorian accent and using Ivorian idioms—requesting *pain au chocolate* and *chocolate chaud* everywhere he goes. Mateo is six and learns to speak with the other kids in the apartment complex by playing soccer with them. Oskar is nine and studies blacksmithing at the outdoor market, reads comic books in English and French, and memorizes poems for extra Minecraft time. The boys and I feel apartment-bound and lonely much of the time—though I speak mediocre to poor French, my accent is not Ivorian, and all interactions (cab rides, purchases, directions) are long-negotiated and impossible for me to do while keeping Archie and Mateo, for example, out of the open sewers they love to play in along the roadsides. So we only go out into Abidjan when Todd can go with us.

A couple months after we arrive we travel north, to the Muslim part of the country, and spend two weeks in Korhogo—this is my favorite part of Cote d'Ivoire. On another trip, Todd's best friend Adam meets us in Abidjan and travels with us to the center of the country where Todd and Adam were in the Peace Corps together. Adam, his wife, his baby daughter, Todd, the boys, our friend Simon and I—we hire a bus to drive us to the village of Zraoulo, where the boys and I finally see where Todd used to live... the hut, the cement porch, the spider-filled latrine, the endless clouds, the indescribably particular smells of fire and food and charcoal and soil, and the fields around the village that Todd has referenced hundreds of times since we've known him.

We see much of Cote d'Ivoire, but our other travel plans in the rest of West Africa are thwarted by the ebola outbreak in neighboring countries, and the uptick of bombings by Boko Haram.

But stuck in the apartment, our psyches unravel.

Winter

I fly back to Los Angeles with the boys a month before Todd returns.
On the flight from Abidjan to Paris, Mateo begins to fever. I am
worried that we will be quarantined in Paris because the world is on
high-alert for ebola. We pass through French airport security, get on
the flight from Paris to Los Angeles, and Archie also begins to fever.
Mateo is at this point so sick on the plane that he shits his pants. I'm
holding Archie, who is very hot and vomiting on me, so Oskar does
his best to help Mateo clean up and change his clothes in the airplane
bathroom. Oskar wipes most of the poop off Mateo's legs, dresses him
in the pajamas I'd brought for the plane ride, and throws away Mateo's
pants in the plane bathroom. By the time we land at LAX, thirty-two
hours after we'd taken off from Abidjan, we all have fevers. I carry
both Mateo and Archie through customs and passport control while
Oskar leans on me, shivering—helping me, as much as he can, push
the two luggage carts filled with our fourteen cardboard boxes
and bags.

We walk, shivering and smelling like shit, out into the crowd at LAX
where Lindy meets us—she's flown in from the peninsula to help me
with the kids in Los Angeles.

The next day Archie and Mateo's fevers are gone. To be on the
safe side I take them to their pediatrician at UCLA. Because we're
returning from West Africa and there's still an active ebola outbreak in
parts of that region, they draw several large vials of blood to test them
for everything under the sun. A few days later, we all feel perfectly
healthy again. The boys are playing legos on the floor with Lindy
while I read aloud to them from *Family Under the Bridge*. In the middle
of the book I receive a phone call from the pediatrician saying I need
to drive Archie to the emergency room *immediately,* that his life hangs
in the balance—that his blood culture had grown a gram-negative
bacteria. I said "but he's feeling perfectly fine—he's playing with his
brothers and eating and laughing." His doctor replies "That's not
possible." His doctor says, at some point, the word "fatal," and I get
him in the car.

I meet his doctor at UCLA Medical Center in Santa Monica where
they admit Archie to their pediatric quarantine unit. When doctors
and nurses enter and leave Archie's room they have to pass through

two sets of special quarantine doors, and they wear light blue hazmat suits with superhero stickers stuck to them—ostensibly to worry Archie less.

At the hospital they do more rounds of blood tests. Archie and I spend three days in the quarantine unit, waiting for the blood cultures to grow—to confirm or deny the presence of the gram-negative bacteria or anything possibly more worrisome. No one is allowed to visit, but infectious diseases doctors move in and out of the room with enthusiasm—Archie's is a high-interest case. He likes the attention because he's bored out of his mind. Eventually the test results come back perfectly normal—the original test, they tell us, must have been a false-positive.

We walk out of the two sets of quarantine doors, and return home.

It is February in Los Angeles.

We have health insurance.

Winter

I returned with the boys to Los Angeles a couple weeks ago, but Todd is still in Abidjan.

Archie is right here next to me. Soft sweet cheeks. The curl of hair at his neck. His little toes, while he sleeps, my god I.

What am I asking. What am I pushing at so hard.

What am I trying to destroy.

Winter

Todd sends pictures in an email from West Africa, from the onboard window of his plane that has been blocked on the runway in Niamey, Niger by a U.S. military cargo plane that is unloading. The military is setting up a base to extend its war on terror. A helicopter is being serviced. Forklifts haul pallets beyond the airport to a storage area with rows and rows of hard-shelled tents.

We are, invisibly to me, bombing someone right now. But what *can* I see right now?: sparkling Christmas tree.

Pretty rug. Todd will be gone a few more weeks. This week he's working with slam poets in Ouagadougou, Burkina Faso.

Then the older one throws blocks at his block tower to topple it and, in doing so, hits his baby brother crawling on the other side of the tower.

The littler one cries, the older one does it again. Then again.

My love, I tell him, check your trajectory.

My love, I tell him, let's be gentle with this baby.

Big guns!, screeches the bigger boy, throwing another block directly at his brother.

And then I'm so fucking pissed I.

Winter

The bed smells like gasoline where their father slept last night. The baby wakes, two bodies over, and says: lawnmower. The older one, half asleep, responds: Who is she? She's beautiful. Their father, half asleep, says Help me, Obi-Wan,

you're my only hope.

Winter

Todd asks what I'm writing. I say well my publisher says it's a book
about dirty centers and maws.

Oh, he says, — it's your book about holding infinite opposite truths
inside of oneself in order to stay on earth.

He hands me a cup of coffee, I.

Winter

Every morning, for so many years, I drink my small cup of coffee very hot, very strong, with a little bit of cream.

At some point while I drink the coffee I think, for a moment, about my father leaving my sister's hospital room to get a cup of coffee, and that's when she died.

Across my life, until just before he died himself, every now and then he'd quietly mention that story as he drank his cup of coffee. My parents knew that Amy's life was ending. She was four years old, and she'd been diagnosed two years earlier with a brain tumor. There was no treatment, just a couple of things they could do to make her more comfortable, like removing part of her skull to relieve the pressure on her brain.

The story he told goes like this—some of the extended family had driven from Nebraska to Wichita, where my dad had his first job out of college, in order to be with my family for the final days of Amy's life. While my young aunts and uncles and my older brothers were dying eggs the evening before Easter, my sister stopped breathing as she slept in my dad's arms. She'd been mostly sleeping for days. My mom placed the hand mirror beneath her nose to see if there was any breath.

There was none, or else her breathing was very slowed, so they rushed her to the hospital.

At the hospital her breathing was assisted. She was alive, but not really, throughout Easter day and night. On the Monday morning after Easter my dad walked down the hall to get a cup of coffee. And that moment, when he left get a cup of coffee, she died.

I was born a few months later.

I love my morning coffee ritual so much that sometimes I joke that I look forward to going to bed at night because I'm that much closer to waking up the next morning, to have a cup of coffee.

Christmas Genital Self-Examination

He is pounding on the door. He wants to use the bathroom.

He is in my arms while I finish typing this on the bathroom floor. He is yelling that he has to poop. Now his diaper is off and he's on the toilet and he is pooping. Now I kneel in front of the toilet and put my arms around him because he is still new to using the toilet and he's afraid of falling in—

when we confront the unknown—and begin to speak.

Christmas Genital Self-Examination

Not weight, but glut.

The—*density*—between this beautiful boy and myself, kneeling as in prayer here before him. As the density of the lights on our Christmas tree right now—too much of all kinds of light, this morning.

This morning Oskar showed me an article about dwindling whale pods off the coast of Los Angeles.

I cannot bear it. I cannot bear—how fragile. Up and down the California coast the navy's sonar exercises, the whales and sea turtles and dolphins and other marine life, their brains exploding and this family-animal—are our brains, right now, exploding we.

I look out of my own eyes, and I want to be a complete mind—here in our bathroom in Venice. Roses outside the window—I can't stop thinking about the salmon who should be outside my window on the peninsula right now—yesterday I spoke with the woman who is now living in our old cabin. She says the salmon never arrived this year—I.

Is the light of this world—a secret.

Christmas Genital Self-Examination

Winter break from their school—the boys are at the beach with Todd this morning.

I want to arrange this book in such a way that whoever reads it knows—there is no hope. There is no arc of redemption.

When did I first have the thought—*if I could be wiped away from earth.*

If my life could stop, like winter stops life, and if I—what would I trade for this earth. What would I trade for the complete minds of the whales. The ancient pathways for salmon.

What of this earth, without me, could then continue. Stones—or doors within us, opening. I want to say the doors inside of me are all open. All the windows are swung wide.

I am pouring or gushing out and—it's raining.

This is a book about mercy, and what might wipe mercy from the face of earth—the earth that I love.

And where I love. And, upon which, I am loved. There is thunder—

complete mind—.

Christmas Genital Self-Examination

I'm not sure why but so much anxiety tonight—it's midnight.
Everyone else is asleep.

Todd's mom suggested that perhaps my vertigo episodes and what I
refer to as anxiety is actually my brains exploding.

From internet news, and wifi, and the massive new connectivity of the
family-animal.

Oskar said perhaps I'm experiencing an outpouring of wartime
revelations—he said I'm writing a "wartime literature."

Mateo said I probably won't be able to meditate for a hundred years.

Archie said: mama what am I supposed to remember?

I said: Remember—don't open your front door until you have
positively identified who is there.

I said: I've seen countless cases where the attacker gains access to his
victims simply by knocking on their door.

I said: Shut the door behind you when you leave.

But first, turn it to the *ocean waves* setting on the sound machine.

Winter

I often say to my students: what does your poem build, and what does your poem destroy?

There should always be something you want to destroy.

I remind my students—what you leave out of your book is as important as what remains in your book.

What am I leaving out of this book—what pieces do I hold up to the light, and then hide back away—.

It's years later, I'm deciding whether or not to keep the lines above.

Oskar and Mateo are hitting each other with books and laughing, right now.

I am screaming: out. Get out. Get out. Get out of here. Right now.

The Snow Man

104.2

103.9

102.1

100.3

This massive new connectivity, my god.

The Snow Man

The collective hundreds of hours of kneeling before them while they learn to use the toilet, touching their adorable knees or holding their backs for balance, because they worry about the water below them.

During these times we are eye to eye, their little nose to my nose, they are touching my face and we are saying sweet things to each other— they might be resting their forehead on mine,

they probably are telling me about a game they've been playing, or raising questions they have about the world—Archie asked me today, for example, as he hovered over the toilet water—why can you die if you fall onto water from high up, but not from down low?

When he is the hero Laser-Flash he will not die when he falls onto the water from high up.

Winter

The children gain language as I.

Archie: Goddamn sonofabitch.
Archie: Fucking god!
Archie: Fucking sonofabitch god shit.
Oskar: Archie say something cute instead.
Archie: ...baby.
Oskar: Say something else cute.
Archie: ...milk.
Oskar: Say something else cute.
Archie: Baby milk.

Winter

Mama I notice you wrote that you "hate Trump with your vulva" yes I did write that.

So could you also say you love someone with your vulva yes you could say that too.

So someone can possibly love or hate someone else with their vulva yes.

Their penis too yes or their ear yes head yes butthole yes earhole yes face yes.

So mama can you love someone with your death star yes can you love someone with your blaster yes can you love someone with your carbonite yes can you love someone with your retinal scanner yes can you love someone with your screen door yes can you love someone with your cup of coffee yes.

But you can't *hate* someone with your cup of coffee can you? yes you can.

Mateo: You can throw it at their face.

The winter after Trump is elected I can't stop thinking about my attacker. I can't stop thinking about my father—how someone so vital and so kind could disappear from earth. I can't stop thinking that winter could disappear from earth. I can't stop thinking about the vertigo that I am now always experiencing or just about to experience. I can't stop thinking about the vulnerability and fragility of animals and forests and oceans and people.

I can't stop thinking of Barthes' footnote about his mother in his *Mourning Diary*:

1. Remember that she lived.

Christmas Genital Self-Examination

Mirrors, if angled just right—

Donald Trump starting from where the shaft and crura meet, and continuing down along the sides of the vestibule, where there are two bundles of erectile tissue called the bulbs of the vestibule, I.

The bulbs, along with the whole clitoris (glans, shaft, crura), become firm and filled with blood during sexual arousal, as do the walls of the vagina where I also.

Donald Trump with my urinary opening I.

Donald Trump vaginal coronas come in widely varying sizes and shapes. For most women they stretch easily—by a tampon, as well as a finger, a penis, or a dildo.

Donald Trump if you're comfortable doing so, slowly put a finger or two inside your vagina. Those are your vaginal walls. If it hurts or if you have trouble, take a deep breath and relax. You may be pushing at an awkward angle, your vagina may be dry, or you may be unconsciously tensing the muscles owing to fear or discomfort. Try shifting positions and using a lubricant such as olive or almond oil (don't use a perfumed oil or lotion that could cause irritation).

Vulva modeled upon the exchanging of property.

Vulva devising a torture system to sell to the CIA for 81 million dollars.

Vulva of the prison industrial system vulva of water boarding vulva according to the logics of global capitalism vulva of disposable populations I.

Vulva fight relentlessly to end exploitation and oppression everywhere, also on your reviled point, vulva.

Donald Trump notice how your vaginal walls, which are touching each other, spread around and hug your fingers.

Feel the soft folds of mucous membrane. These folds allow the vagina to stretch and to mold itself around whatever is inside, including fingers, a tampon, a penis, a dildo, or your baby during childbirth.

ExxonMobil with my vaginal walls I.

ExxonMobil with my vaginal and my cervical discharge.

Monsanto and ExxonMobil about a third of the way up from my vaginal opening, on the anterior wall of the vagina, in an area known as the Gräfenberg spot, or G-spot.

Monsanto and ExxonMobil push gently against the walls of your vagina, and notice where the walls feel particularly sensitive to touch. This sensitivity may occur only in the area closest to the vaginal opening, or in most or all of the vagina and I.

Donald Trump my fornix is the thin wall of mucous membrane and connective tissue that separates my vagina from my rectum.

Donald Trump you may be able to feel bumps on the back side of my vagina if I have some stool in my rectum.

ExxonMobil slide your middle finger as far back into your vagina as you can. Notice that your finger goes in toward the small of your back at an angle, not straight up the middle of your body. If you were standing, your vagina would be at about a 45-degree angle to the floor.

With your finger you may be able to just feel the deep end of your vagina, or the fornix.

Donald Trump not everyone can reach this— it may help if you bring your knees and chest closer together so your finger can slide in farther.

ExxonMobil a little before the end of your vagina you can feel your cervix.

Donald Trump your cervix feels like a nose with a small dimple in its center. The cervix (from the Latin cervix uteri, meaning "neck of the womb") is the part of the uterus that extends into your vagina where I.

ExxonMobil the entrance is very small. Normally, only menstrual fluid leaving the uterus, or seminal fluid entering the uterus, passes through the cervix that I.

No tampon, finger, dildo, or penis can go up through my cervix, although it is capable of expanding enormously for a baby during labor and birth.

Vulva, rows of teeth at our jugular.

Vulva, the warmth of your breath, the smell of your blood.

Vulva, ask me about when it.

Vulva, it irritated me that he should force a nasty little brat like me to understand.

Vulva, I could not risk learning.

Vulva, my grubby little hands dangled at my sides.

Vulva, you were unattainable.

Vulva, I became the immensity of calm, the elimination of the, the joining of the, the rapture at the, the death of the, the loss in the face of the.

Vulva, look at something you don't understand for a long time, and it will change you.

Hyper-awareness I— Monsanto.

Monsanto my anus, which you pass through.

Monsanto my anus, from which you emerge new into the world.

Monsanto—the immeasurable kindness of my anus.

When you do a self-examination, make sure you have enough time and privacy to feel relaxed.

ExxonMobil try squatting on the floor and putting a hand-mirror between your feet.

ExxonMobil if you're uncomfortable in that position, sit as far forward on the edge of a chair as you comfortably can, separate your legs, and place the mirror between them.

ExxonMobil you give me the oil to make the bright blue plastic frame around the hand-mirror that I squat over.

The bleached wood pulp, and the cotton that makes the tampon which I.

ExxonMobil you give me the plastic wrap around the tampon that I.

Donald Trump if you're having a hard time seeing, try aiming a flashlight at your genitals, or aiming a flashlight at the mirror that you are squatting over.

Donald Trump squat. Shine the light. Look into the mirror.

Monsanto, look so far up inside that you can see your own heart, beating yourself to death.

Vulva-related ideas, vulva beholders, vulva at the sucking portal, vulva legend that just glided past him, vulva's impartial eyesight, vulva's investigative eye, vulva drawing Constantinople for her sons, vulva's treat, vulva eating chocolate croissants with her sons this morning, vulva the homogeneous totality of darkness, vulva verbalizes the indescribable cave, vulva of the all-too-familiar, vulva's analytical intelligence, vulva's exquisite night, vulva playing language games, vulva becoming increasingly self-conscious as her son reads over her shoulder while she writes about vulvas, vulva is that the part outside mama yes sweetie, vulva the one part of me that is not always talking about contained-ness, vulva the reality of the pioneer, vulva closely following the market, vulva makes an ink drawing of the mouth of hell.

Vulva, pulverizes her sweetness, and feeds it to her children.

Christmas Poem

Stop. Stop it.

Stop hitting me with Dark Vader while I poop.

Winter

The children smack my head as they bash my computer. The youngest has shit on his hands because he finally wiped his own butt.

There is nothing I wouldn't steal or destroy for them. There is no tree on earth I'd spare. There is no throat I wouldn't shit down I.

I'd impale myself. On that poker over there by the fireplace. Then jerk around to enlarge the opening. So they could better devour my.

The insidiousness of how I love them. The family-animal is holy to me, and being their mother has changed my brains. Has given me a kind of soul, I.

What would it mean to a reader who doesn't love me to know that I have *never hoped to transcend*—that I want to descend.

I want to entrench—to dig into the childhoods of my children, and to stop—right there. I want to melt at the feet of the children.

I want to be absorbed into the ground below their feet, then be sucked up by a tree.

I want that tree to be logged, turned into lumber, and sold back to me.

I want to use those boards that I just bought to build a deck that I can sit on,

and watch myself fall back down at night in the form of snow.

Or, better, fall directly into the open mouths of my children.

The Snow Man

It's a beautiful summer in Venice. We're living about six blocks from the beach, and we spend most our afternoons there.

I'm about three years in to having these vertigo episodes. Archie is three.

Emerson said for every seeing soul there are two absorbing facts, —*I and the Abyss.*

Whitman said he contains multitudes.

Stevens once said: I shall explain *The Snow Man* as an example of the necessity of identifying oneself with reality in order to understand it and enjoy it.

But I'm so much more interested when Joyelle McSweeney says I want to see a renovating spear split and kill me from its eye. Is this the year I'll be born?

I have also been re-reading Song of Songs and Ecclesiastes and Enheduanna and Sappho and the gnostic gospels and Paul Clean and a biography of Clarice Lispector and Roland Barthes' *Mourning Diary,* which he wrote after his beloved mother died.

I have been—even more than there already is, inside of my brains, I—

my dad died two and a half years ago.

Winter

As I was saying. Stevens once said: I shall explain *The Snow Man* as an example of the necessity of identifying oneself with reality in order to understand it and enjoy it.

But I'm so much more interested when Clarice Lispector says Death takes place in my very being—how can I explain to you?

I am so much more interested when Psalm 22:14 says I am poured out like water. My bones are scattered. And my heart, like wax, is melted. In the midst of my bowels.

I am so much more interested when Audre Lorde says The difference between poetry and rhetoric is being ready to kill yourself instead of your children.

I have my cup of coffee and the sand on our bed is making the keys of my computer crunch a little bit each time I press the keys. It's 3 a.m.

I am so much more interested when Dolores Dorantes and Rodrigo Flores Sánchez say I am not a good person all I am is my country.

I am so much more interested when Jean Valentine says wildwood mother you fill my center-hole with bliss no one is so tender in her scream.

I am so much more importantly-dislocated when Lucille Clifton says the terror is in the plain pink at the window and the hedges moral as fire and the plain face of the white woman watching us as she beats her ordinary bread I.

Christmas, Montana, my dad has been dead for about three years

Okay, Archie count to forty while we hide. 1, 2, 3, 4, 5, 6, 7, 9, 14, 16, 11, 9. Ready or not here I come 6, 7, 8, sixty-four-eleven-nine-forty! Ready or not here I come 14, 18, hey mama what are you doing?

By the time a child crawls he is blanketed by an enormous, unseen cloud of microorganisms—a hundred trillion or more bacteria viruses yeasts fungi.

All told the child's body holds about 3 pounds of microorganisms— about the same as the weight of his brain mama what are you doing on your computer?

They congregate in his digestive system and mouth and fill the spaces between his teeth cover his skin line his throat. The cells of microorganisms outnumber those we consider to be his own cells by 10 to 1.

What did you say mama? I said I am trying to write about what is inside of us, Archie. What did you say mama? I am trying to write about what is inside of us, Archie.

What are you even saying to me mama? I am trying to show what love does to a mind.

I can't hear what you necessarily mean mama.

Winter

What are we possibly going to eat—what food would you actually eat
if I set it before you? Egg.

Are you *actually* going to eat an egg, my love, or just *theoretically* eat it?
Theoretically, mama.

Their father says: please consider this coffee as an alternative
to suicide.

Winter

I don't know how to stop making this book.

The children are at the beach with friends this morning. The three of them walked out the front door laughing and they didn't look back—not even Archie, and he's only four.

Has individuation stolen all my symbolic gifts—

my dad died four and a half years ago. Is it possible, sufficiently, to grow apart from each other, far enough to think—I.

I'm writing a book about a book that is no longer here—as my children are no longer here—they are *there* now.

They are over there, next to the water, digging holes in the sand. They are right next to the ocean, laughing with their friends, and they are completely outside of me.

We are, mostly, all outside of each other.

This book is, mostly, outside of me. So many different kinds of books it has been, or could still be, apart from me.

Over there. Right there.

Winter

This morning I am drinking my coffee in bed in Donegal, Ireland. I'll be gone from home for two weeks to teach. I'm still jet-lagged and not sure what time I—Todd is texting, taking dictation, he is putting the children to bed:

Birth of my love mama I miss you please come back from Archie.

Winter

Am I seeking consolation—the years are now just—*time*. Their bodies
are just human bodies.

Look: there's the wooden gun that each of my babies loved in their
mouths when they were teething,

Winter

Where once we had animals and seasons, now we have—. As the earth warms, humanity's accumulated wisdom about the earth—the seasons, the landscape, the animals—becomes progressively less effective as a guide to the future.

Civilization enters a dark age in its practical understanding of our planet. Where do we go when,

what do we do, what does it mean that *we live on earth,* and when we approach or are approached by—how do we—.

When asking for directions and someone offers to show you the way by telling you to follow them, do *not* go along. Just ask them to point you in the right direction—then go the other way.

Often, predators just want to get you to a less crowded place, where your screams can't be heard.

Winter

What do we attach our anxieties to—what are the exact contours of a swarm?

What do we attach our anxieties to, if we separate the globe at its delicate joints.

If we pull the globe apart, gently, to gently to reveal the. The mental shell—

and inside of that, the—. How do I stop this.

How do I stop this book. How do I end this book. I talk with the children about it. I tell them it's a book about long-term grieving tangled up with the deepest joy and wonder I have ever experienced—and my own mind's explosion. Then possible re-composure. I tell them it's about the end of winter on earth, as I have understood winter. It's about the end of their childhoods. It's about the invisible wars. It's about the brains of whales exploding all around earth. I tell them I want to stop writing the book. I tell them I want the book to end, but I don't know how.

Ambivalent, Oskar says, means having purchase in both directions. Ambi, he says, means both. And valent is from the Latin meaning strength. What about a pluripotent feeling to the ending instead, he says. Or a *frozen hesitation*—and that's all that is left of winter.

Mateo suggests the ending of the book feels first like confusion, and then it just dwindles away. Because that, he says, is what we really have been like, growing up.

Archie responds to my questions by describing his nightmare from the night before. He'd woken up crying but he didn't want to tell me about the dream because, he said, it was too terrible. He tells me now:

Mama you are stuck in a chair because you put the seatbelt around your head, and the seatbelt will tighten forever and you are paralyzed, frozen to the chair. And no matter how much I scream for the seatbelt to stop squeezing your head, you are afraid, and you will always be frozen in the chair.

Tomorrow, I think I simply won't sit back down here. Tomorrow, I think, I just won't try again.

Epilogue

Winter

Another dark winter morning and I am alone at my desk. There is a window above my desk, but I can see nothing except myself, my cup of coffee, the living room behind me, dimly lit by the fire. There is a new moon, so it is extremely dark outside.

I press my face against the glass—a half-circle of snow on the ground is illuminated by my lamp.

Above the illuminated half-circle, there is illuminated, also, a wedge of snow, thickly falling.

It is falling—*excruciatingly slowly.*

In the quiet. In my brains. In this darkness. I have a thought. I can hear it:

my thought it is so soft,

my thought it is so thick,

my thought it is so slow,

it is—suspended. My thought is: *tenderness.* It is: *console.* It is:

the fire is burning, there is a cup of coffee in front of me, I am having a thought:

I am so happy.

Acknowledgements

I received depths of help, guidance, ideas, reads, talks, insights, and love while writing this book over thirteen years—thank you:

Todd Fredson, Oskar, Mateo, Archie.

Thank you Carmen Giménez Smith, Emily Alex, Sarah Gzemski, Alban Fischer.

Thank you Prageeta Sharma, Alicia Ostriker, Jenny Boully.

Thank you Rachel Zucker, Danielle Pafunda, Bonnie Nadzam, Sherwin Bitsui, Sean Nevin, James McHugh, Henry Quintero, Ross Gay, Norman Dubie, Cynthia Hogue, Matthew Gavin Frank, Sally Ball, Dexter Booth, Mary Bergstrom, Forrest Gander, C.D. Wright, Robin Coste Lewis, Diana Arterian, David St. John, Douglas Manuel, Joshua Rathkamp, Natasha Murdock, Tanya Brown Merriman, Emily Anderson, Alice Gambrell, David Treuer, Aracelis Girmay, Afaa Michael Weaver, Ellen Doré Watson, Oliver de la Paz, Liz Weld, Diana Park, Arielle Greenberg, Susan Briante, Farid Matuk, Janalynn Bliss, Virginia Konchan, Jeff Encke, Hallie Mueller, Lori and Adam Boyd, Kim and Josh Robison, Alissa McGonigal, Elizabyth Hiscox, Douglas Jones, Joy Katz, Judith Vollmer, Aimee Nezhukumatathil, Mihaela Moscaliuc, Michael Waters, Matthew Gavin Frank, Debra Earling, Marci Vogel, Mark Irwin, Ruth Ellen Kocher, Rosa Alcalá, Christopher Freeman, Hoa Nguyen, Carmen Hoover, Dawn Pichon Barron, Patrick Finn, Valerie Bandura, Maggie Nelson.

Thank you to University of Southern California, University of Montana, and Drew University—and especially to my students.

Thank you Linda Vap, Daniel Vap, Lindy Parker and Mike Fredson, for watching over us.

Thank you to those of you who loved, taught, and helped me while our children were little together.